Amados Compatriotas

Frontispiece. "Memoria de la Secretaria de Estado y de Despacho Relaciones Interiores y Exteriores (January 7–8, 1831)." Myra Ellen Jenkins, *Calendar of the Mexican Archives of New Mexico, 1821–1846* (State of New Mexico Records Center, 1970). 1830 Governor's Papers. Communications received from Secretaría de Estado.

amados compatriotas

And Other Stories from New Mexico's Mexican Period, 1821–1846

Robert J. Tórrez

UNIVERSITY OF NEW MEXICO PRESS
ALBUQUERQUE

Printed in the United States of America

Library of Congress Cataloging-in-Publication Data

Names: Tórrez, Robert J. author
Title: Amados compatriotas : and other stories from New Mexico's Mexican period, 1821–1846 / Robert J. Tórrez.
Other titles: Beloved fellow patriots | Mexican archives of New Mexico, 1821–1846
Description: Albuquerque : University of New Mexico Press, 2026.
Identifiers: LCCN 2025054773 | ISBN 9780826369598 paperback | ISBN 9780826369604 epub
Subjects: LCSH: Mexican archives of New Mexico, 1821–1846 | New Mexico—History—To 1848 | BISAC: HISTORY / United States / 19th Century | HISTORY / Latin America / Mexico
Classification: LCC F800 .T67 2026 | DDC 978.903—dc23/eng/20260113
LC record available at https://lccn.loc.gov/2025054773

Founded in 1889, the University of New Mexico sits on the traditional homelands of the Pueblo of Sandia. The original peoples of New Mexico—Pueblo, Navajo, and Apache—since time immemorial have deep connections to the land and have made significant contributions to the broader community statewide. We honor the land itself and those who remain stewards of this land throughout the generations and also acknowledge our committed relationship to Indigenous peoples. We gratefully recognize our history.

Cover illustration by Isaac Morris
Designed by Isaac Morris
Composed in Adobe Jenson, Covik sans, Luminari, and Neue Haas Grotesque.

Contents

Introduction

"*Amados Compatriotas*"—Beloved Fellow Patriots. With these words Alejo García Conde, Commanding General of the Internal Provinces of the West, advised New Mexicans that Mexico's long and difficult struggle for independence from Spain was over and called for the unity that would be needed to sustain and nourish their newfound liberty. The full text of García Conde's message and a brief outline of New Mexico's introduction to Mexican independence will be found in the opening chapter.

García Conde's message opens roll one of the *Calendar of the Mexican Archives of New Mexico 1821–1846*.[1] The Mexican Archives of New Mexico consist of forty-three rolls of microfilm containing thousands of administrative, military, judicial, and financial records that tell us much about the brief but defining twenty-five years during which New Mexico transitioned from being part of the Spanish Empire to a short-lived Mexican Empire and finally, a nascent republic, before being assumed as a territory of the United States. This documentary treasure encompasses the correspondence and reports of governors and myriad government officials that provide the minutiae of governance. These include numerous records that describe New Mexico's often contentious relations, and the constant state of war it endured, with the native peoples who inhabited and surrounded the often-beleaguered territory. And of some importance, the countless details of the impact of trappers, adventurers, entrepreneurs, and traders who made their way to New Mexico over the Santa Fe Trail as soon as independence was achieved, and subsequently, how the nascent Mexican government struggled to regulate and control this trade while growing increasingly dependent on the revenue it produced.

The sixty-three essays published here first appeared as monthly columns beginning with the November 6, 1992, issue of *Santa Fe Pride*, a bimonthly newspaper published by the late Amy Manning. Amy approached me while I was still serving as the New Mexico state historian at the State Records Center and Archives in Santa Fe and asked if I would contribute a regular column about New Mexico history and its historic characters. This was an opportunity I had sought for some time, a task that fit well with the state historian's role in enhancing the public's knowledge and appreciation of New Mexico's history and its cultural resources—especially those priceless documentary resources that constitute our Spanish, Mexican, and Territorial-era archives.

I also had in mind a title for the column—"Voices From the Past." I often say the title comes from the real and imagined noises that emanated from the old joists and overloaded wooden floors of the warehouse and basement that constituted the archive vault at the old Ilfeld warehouse on the corner of Montezuma Avenue and Guadalupe Street in Santa Fe, where the original State Records Center and Archives was established in the early 1960s. In my imagination, however, the countless pages of letters, reports, and ledgers that filled the archive shelves, some dating back to the seventeenth century, whispered to me that they had countless stories to tell: voices from the past, straining to be heard.

In 1998 the State Records Center and Archives was transferred from the old building on Montezuma to the new, state-of-the-art Governor Garrey Carruthers building on

Camino Carlos Rey, which also houses the New Mexico State Library. At the new facility, the chain and padlock that secured the rickety sliding door to the basement vault was replaced with an electronically activated lock that allows entry into a clean, well-lit, modern storage vault. When the door is opened, there is a sort of "whoosh," a rush of air caused by the difference in air pressure between the entrance hall and the dedicated HVAC system that controls the temperature and humidity of the vault where the archives are kept. When I first heard that sound, it seemed as if all those voices that simply groaned and whispered at the old location had awakened and now shouted with a sort of refreshing glee—voices that beckoned us to enter and discover anew the endless variety of untold stories of the little-known or forgotten aspects of New Mexico's history and the people that lived it.

"Voices From the Past" columns appeared regularly in *Santa Fe Pride* until February 1996, when the paper ceased publication. Soon afterward, Gerard and Janet Iff asked me to continue the monthly articles for *Round the Roundhouse: New Mexico State Employees' Newspaper,* and the column resumed in this new venue with the August 29, 1996, issue. The column has since achieved several milestones: the one-hundredth column in 2002; number two hundred little less than a decade later, in 2010; and by the time this volume is published, the column will have surpassed three decades of publication and more than three hundred columns as *Round the Roundhouse* continues under the ownership of the late John Hetzler and his wife, Carol.

Amados Compatriotas is the fourth volume of the "Voices From the Past" monthly columns the author has published in

Santa Fe Pride and *Round the Roundhouse* since 1992. The first volume, now out of print, was published in 2004 by the University of New Mexico Press. It is a compilation of thirty-seven early columns under the title *UFOs Over Galisteo and Other Stories of New Mexico History*. The title comes from an 1880 newspaper story about the reported sighting of "A Mysterious Aerial Phantom" in the sky above Galisteo, southeast of Santa Fe. A second volume of "Voices From the Past" columns was published in 2017 by Rio Grande Books under the title *Voices From the Past: The Comanche Raid of 1776 & Other Tales of New Mexico History*. This second volume of "Voices" columns has earned critical acclaim: It was recognized as the best anthology at the 2018 New Mexico-Arizona Book Awards and was awarded first place in the Non-Fiction, Best History Book category from Latino Literacy Now, a prestigious nonprofit organization co-founded in 1997 by Edward James Olmos and Kirk Whisler. The third volume, *New Mexico's Wicked City & Other True Stories of New Mexico History* followed, in 2024. The title of Wicked City is taken from a traveler's description of New Mexico's major cities and his dismay over the numerous saloons, dancehalls, gambling, and other unnamed "entertainments" he observed. *New Mexico's Wicked City* has also been selected by the 2024 New Mexico-Arizona Book Awards as the Best New Mexico History: Anthology.

These three volumes have featured a broad variety of topics taken from New Mexico's Spanish (1598–1821), Mexican (1821–1846), and Territorial (1846–1912) eras along with a few from the Statehood (1912 to present) period. Of the more than three hundred published "Voices From the Past" columns, approximately a third have featured topics taken from New Mexico's brief twenty-five-year Mexican era. Some of these Mexican-era columns have appeared in the three previous books but *Amados Compatriotas* consists exclusively of material found in the vast and little-used documentary treasure that is New Mexico's Mexican-era archives. Each chapter provides a peek into aspects of the executive, administrative, judicial, commercial, and military workings of a government that struggled mightily to transition from a monarchy to a republic.

The reader is cautioned not to expect *Amados Compatriotas* to be a comprehensive history of New Mexico's Mexican period. Many volumes will be required to produce a competent history of the events and personalities of this important period of New Mexico's history. There is so much material available in our Mexican-era archives that many of these columns could be developed into their own volume. Suffice to say that topics covered by many of these columns have never been published before and provide insight into little-known elements of the era's history.

As I noted in the previous volumes, these articles do not have footnotes. However, every column has enough dates, names, and other information that those interested in following up or verifying details about the topic should easily find its source in the microfilm version of the Mexican Archives of New Mexico, 1821–1846, which is available at the New Mexico State Records Center and Archives, all major universities in the state, and several public libraries, as well as online through Ancestry.com.

Readers who may want to delve deeper into this crucial period of New Mexico history have a limited choice of published sources. Within that limited selection one can start with the early publication of Lansing B. Bloom's 1913–1914 *Old Santa Fe* series on "New Mexico Under Mexican Administration 1822–1846." Much more recent and more readily available is David J. Weber's *The Mexican Frontier, 1821–1846: The American Southwest Under Mexico.* This comprehensive work provides a history of New Mexico within the context of the broader Southwest and the Spanish- and Mexican-era institutions that constituted present-day New Mexico, Arizona, Texas, and California. Of the few books specific to New Mexico for the period, Janet Lecompte's *Rebellion in Rio Arriba, 1837* is highly recommended. Published in 1985, Lecompte's extensive use of primary documents makes this a reliable source for study of the critical events of that year. Jill Mocho's groundbreaking *Murder and Justice in Frontier New Mexico, 1821–1846* is a valuable source that delves into how the Mexican-era judicial system functioned, and tragically, how it often failed to achieve justice. Martín González de la Vara's research into the era's financial records is an invaluable resource, although his publications are available only in scholarly journals and in Spanish.

Among the dozens of books by and about the merchants, trappers, and adventurers that came to New Mexico during the Mexican era, Josiah Gregg's *Commerce of the Prairies* remains, despite its Anglo-centric leanings, an important source about commerce along the Santa Fe Trail. For the role of Hispano merchants in the Santa Fe Trail trade, I suggest Susan Calafate Boyle's *Los Capitalistas, Hispano Merchants and the Santa Fe Trade.*

For decades, the Fray Angélico Chávez trilogy on New Mexico's influential clergy, Padre José Antonio Martínez (*But*

Time and Chance: The Story of Padre Martínez, 1793–1867), José Manuel Gallegos (*Très Macho—He Said*), and Juan Felipe Ortiz (*Wake for a Fat Vicar*), enhanced the general lack of published biography on New Mexico's influential Mexican-era leadership. The early chapters of Marc Simmons's *The Little Lion of the Southwest: A Life of Manuel Antonio Chaves* and Jacqueline Dorgan Meketa's *Legacy of Honor: The Life of Rafael Chacón, A Nineteenth-Century New Mexican* delve briefly into the Mexican era. The recent publication by Maurilio E. Vigil and Helene Boudreau, *Donaciano Vigil: The Life of a Nuevomexicano Soldier, Statesman, and Territorial Governor* is a welcome and important addition to this short biographical list. As of this publication, one hopes some bold scholar will delve into the life of three-time governor Manuel Armijo, arguably the most influential and important character of this critical era of New Mexico history. Until that time one can reference the various articles on Armijo published by scholars Janet Lecompte, Daniel Tyler, and others in journals such as *Journal of the West* and *New Mexico Historical Review*.

Note

1. Myra Ellen Jenkins, *Calendar of the Mexican Archives of New Mexico, 1821–1846*, State of New Mexico Records Center, 1970.

CHAPTER ONE

Meanwhile, Back at the Villa

The Santa Fe Plaza: A Witness to History

Few public spaces and buildings in the United States can boast of the long and colorful history of New Mexico's Palace of the Governors and its adjacent plaza. The palace can trace its beginnings to 1610, when the Spanish government moved its capital from San Gabriel, which was located on the west bank of Rio Grande across from San Juan Pueblo (Ohkay Owingeh), to the newly established *villa de Santa Fe*. During the past four centuries the buildings, which constituted the *casas reales*—the royal houses of which the palace was a part—have undergone so many changes that we have only a general idea what they may have looked like three hundred years ago. The buildings where the palace now sits were significantly altered, if not destroyed, during the Pueblo Revolt of 1680, occupied and adapted by the Tanos during the subsequent decade into what was described as a "fortress-pueblo" and rebuilt by the Spanish following the *reconquista* of 1693. Indications are, the palace even had a second story in the early eighteenth century. Several major reconstructions followed during the subsequent three centuries, culminating in the last major renovation in 1913, when the palace attained its current appearance.

During the past centuries the palace has served as the home and seat of government for a long succession of Spanish, Mexican, and American officials. Its rooms housed legislatures and court proceedings and provided offices for governors and countless government officials, cells for criminals, and even a bank. For a few weeks in 1862, the Confederate flag flew over this venerable old building. If walls had ears and were capable of speaking, these palace walls would have some marvelous stories to tell!

The palace and its adjoining plaza have been a constant witness to Santa Fe's history. However, the plaza was where much of what was enacted inside the palace was carried out. If a decree was issued, it was announced in the plaza. Imagine an open space that may have extended from Saint Frances Cathedral west to today's Eldorado Hotel and from La Fonda north to the federal courthouse and post office. Every indication is that today's plaza is a mere remnant of the original.

Much of what was significant in New Mexico history took place within this space. Here, the survivors of the initial onslaught of the 1680 Pueblo Revolt sought refuge and resisted the Pueblo siege until they were forced to retreat to Paso del Norte, where they remained in exile until don Diego de Vargas's reconquista. It was within this space that Vargas met with Pueblo leadership and negotiated the "peaceful reconquest" in 1692. It is also the space where the Spanish and the Pueblo Indians clashed when Vargas returned with colonists and missionaries in 1693, and the peaceful reconquest turned bloody.

It is within this space that the minutiae of government took place for more than three centuries. Here, citizens gathered at the call of the military drummer (*el tambor*) to hear the latest news and the most recent proclamations issued by a distant

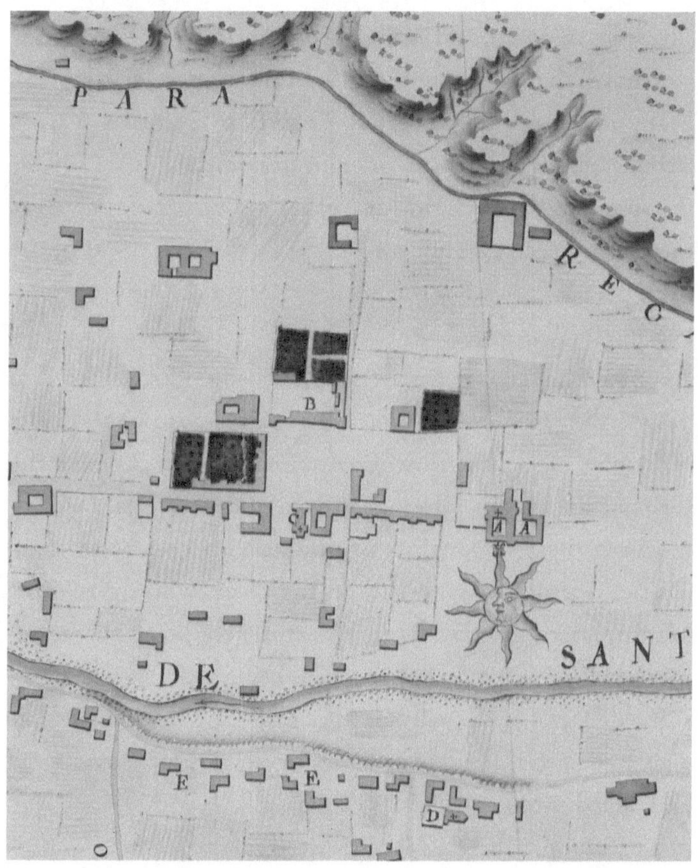

Figure 1. Detail of Joseph Urrutia's 1767 map of Santa Fe showing the plaza and surrounding buildings. The item labeled "B" is the present Palace of the Governors. Courtesy of the British Library, London. Asset No. 084065.

sovereign in Spain, and delivered by couriers who made their way north from Mexico along the camino real (royal road). Here, for example, Governor Francisco Cuervo y Valdés publicly published a royal order on Sunday, May 29, 1705, "at the sound of the war drum and other military instruments at the door of the royal houses and at the four entrances of the royal plaza, by word of the official crier proclaimed in a loud and intelligible voice."

Here the military garrison and citizen militia gathered to answer the call to muster and organize the seemingly endless series of campaigns against the Apaches, Navajos, Utes, or the Comanches. In this same space, government officials accommodated these same tribes to negotiate and celebrate peace treaties. Picture campfires lit on the plaza, where dozens of Native Americans were encamped, and sheep being butchered, meals being cooked, and hot tortillas being made on a comal (a stone or metal grill)—all dutifully paid for from the *fondo de aliados,* a special fund designated for expenditures associated with allied tribes.

Here too, in 1821, a rider arrived carrying official notices informing New Mexicans they were no longer subjects of the Spanish king but were now a part of the nascent Mexican Republic (technically, the Mexican Empire). Here, on September 17, 1821, Governor Facundo Melgares gathered Santa Fe's municipal and military officers to conduct a solemn ceremony in which they pledged allegiance to their new government.

Here too, another change of government took place. On August 19, 1846, the day after General Stephen Watts Kearny and the American Army of the West occupied Santa Fe, Juan Bautista Vigil y Alarid stepped forward and delivered one of the most poignant and famous speeches in New Mexico history as he surrendered New Mexico to its uncertain future. We can only imagine the emotions that flooded over Vigil y Alarid and any assembled citizens as he stood before General Kearny and his troops and marked the end of an era in New Mexico history.

It would take many volumes to chronicle the events that took place within the walls of the Palace of the Governors and the open space of its adjacent plaza. These events are an integral part of New Mexico's most venerable public space and may serve as a too brief reminder of the extraordinary stories that silent voices from the past could tell.

New Mexico's Introduction to Mexican Independence

Mexico celebrates the birth of its independence movement—its Fourth of July—on September 16. This pivotal moment in Mexican history is attributed to Miguel Hidalgo y Costilla, a priest in the parish of Dolores, a small town in what is now the State of Querétaro. On the night of September 15–16, 1810, Padre Hidalgo issued what is called the *Grito de Dolores,* powerful words that sparked a movement that culminated in Mexican independence in 1821, when the Plan of Iguala, the Mexican Declaration of Independence, was recognized by Spain.

There were numerous documents that reached New Mexico advising local officials that Mexican independence had been achieved. One of the most dramatic is the August 27, 1821, decree issued at Chihuahua by Alejo García Conde, the "Comandante

General of the Internal Provinces of the West," in which García Conde addresses his "Beloved Fellow Patriots." This document constitutes the first item listed in the *Calendar of the Mexican Archives of New Mexico, 1821–1846*. While there is no indication when it was received in Santa Fe it might be considered New Mexico's first official notice of the news that New Mexico was now a part of an independent Mexico. The following translation is my own:

> The Commanding General of the Internal Provinces of the West, to the Inhabitants of these:
>
> Beloved Fellow Patriots: The hallowed day providence has designated for the Independence of our country to cross the ocean has arrived. The immortal hero, don Agustín de Yturbide, and the general support of the towns, aware in the most energetic manner throughout New Spain, raises and consolidates at the same time the grand edifice of our liberty. It is not possible to tell of the benefits that we, and principally our successors, will obtain from this work, that blessed by the Almighty, is founded in the basic rights it concedes to all men. The Holy Religion we profess is upheld in the most solid manner. Justice is inseparable from the institutions it has as a foundation, as the sciences, prosperity of commerce and the advance of agriculture and the arts are necessarily the fruits of a liberal government that is based on a healthy morality and a solid foundation of justice; But beloved fellow patriots, it is necessary that we now have a firm adherence to the authorities, an inseparable union of our spirits, and the most resolute determination to shed from our hearts even the faintest trace

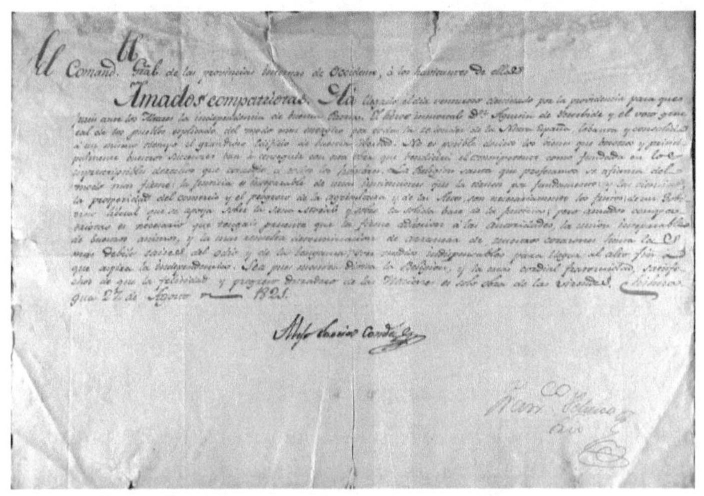

El Comand.te Gral. de las provincias internas de Occidente, á los habitantes de ellas

Amados compatriotas.

Figure 2. Alejo García Conde, Proclamation, August 27, 1821. Myra Ellen Jenkins, *Calendar of the Mexican Archives of New Mexico, 1821–1846* (State of New Mexico Records Center, 1970. Hereafter cited as MANM). 1821 Governor's Papers, Communications received.

of hate and vengeance; These are the indispensable means by which we will reach the pinnacle to which Independence aspires.

Let therefore Religion be our badge [banner], and the most cordial fraternity, satisfied that happiness and lasting progress of nations is solely work of the virtues.

Chihuahua, 27 of August of 1821.

Alejo García Conde

Another document to reach New Mexico advising local officials of Mexican independence is a September 9, 1821, manifesto from Durango that reported the *grito de libertad* (shout of liberty) had been announced at Iguala, calling for the unity that would be required to retain their hard-earned independence. Governor Facundo Melgares noted that the manifesto was copied locally on October 28, but there is no indication if that was the date on which it was received in Santa Fe.

One of the earliest official acknowledgments of Mexican independence by local officials was an order dated August 27 that local officials were to take an oath in honor of "*la Independencia*." Governor Melgares indicated that the order had arrived in Santa Fe on September 17, 1821, a date that suggests this may have been part of the García Conde message cited above. Melgares responded promptly that he had gathered Santa Fe's ayuntamiento (municipal council) and conducted the allegiance ceremony in the presence of the military chaplain, local clerics, and the community, with "all the solemnity possible." He also indicated that the order had been circulated to the *alcaldías* (local political jurisdictions) throughout the province.

This document does not specify the cordillera, or route, by which the order was circulated in New Mexico. However, another document, a copy of an August 9, 1821, proclamation from La Puebla entitled *Triunfo de la Libertad Mexicana* (Triumph of Mexican Liberty) relayed the latest information on the independence movement throughout New Mexico via the typical marginal notation that specifies the route (cordillera) by which the document was circulated and published. This marginal note is important because it suggests which communities were seats of the alcaldías at this time. Couriers delivered the La Puebla document from the capital at Santa Fe to Santa Cruz de la Cañada, proceeded to San Juan de los Caballeros, Abiquiú, Taos, San Miguel del Bado, Cochiti, Alameda, Albuquerque, Isleta, Belen, Laguna, and finally, to the Pueblo of Jemez. By mid-November 1821, several additional circulars regarding independence were being distributed to the alcaldías throughout New Mexico, including copies of the Treaty of Cordova, a surviving copy of which was noted, received, and copied at Santa Cruz de la Cañada on November 17, 1821.

These and numerous additional documents make it clear that New Mexicans were kept well informed of developments in Mexico, which may account for New Mexico's apparent seamless transition from a Spanish province to a part of the nascent Mexican Republic.

The earliest documented public celebration related to Mexican independence in New Mexico took place on January 6, 1822. On that day, after mass, there was a procession, dancers from the Pueblo of Tesuque entertained the crowd, and a dramatic poem (*loa*) was performed by the *alférez* (standard bearer) Santiago Abreu, vicar Juan Tomás Terrazas, and presidio (military garrison) chaplain Fray Francisco de Hozio. The procession was led by a young boy holding a sword in his hand, symbolizing the Plan of Iguala, followed by three girls bound together by a tricolor ribbon, symbolizing the three guarantees of the Plan—Independence, Religion, and Union. After Pueblo Indian dances on the plaza, the crowd dispersed to a variety of games and entertainment and that evening, a dance attended by the city's "persons of distinction" followed at the Palace of the Governors and lasted until four thirty in the morning. The ladies in attendance wore green sashes with "Viva la Independencia del Imperio Mexicano" (Long Live the Independence of the Mexican Empire) imprinted on them.

In the spring of 1822, the recently installed provincial *diputación* (legislative council) drafted a resolution supporting Agustín de Iturbide's Imperial government. The resolution assured their superiors in Mexico that New Mexico's citizens considered themselves an integral and loyal part of the new nation and were prepared to shed their blood in defense of the established government. This resolution also contains a succinct acknowledgment that they considered themselves citizens of a greater America—using the terms "*America Septentorial*," (North Americans) and "*estos leales Americanos*," (these loyal Americans), when referring to themselves.

The Iturbide Celebration of 1822

New Mexico's late Spanish and early Mexican period archives make it clear that local officials were kept well informed of developments while Mexico made its often-painful journey toward independence from Spain. Within weeks of the events that resulted in Mexican independence, Governor Facundo Melgares was distributing the latest news to local officials throughout the territory. So it was when Agustín de Iturbide was proclaimed Imperial Emperor, as 1821 came to a close. A year later, in December 1822, officials in Santa Fe organized a grand celebration to commemorate the first anniversary of Iturbide's inauguration as "first Mexican constitutional emperor."

The Iturbide celebration opened in Santa Fe on the evening of December 10, 1822. The occasion was marked by prayers, bonfires, music, ringing of bells, and discharges of artillery and firearms. A white flag emblazoned "with inscriptions of independence" was hoisted on a very tall pole erected at the center of the plaza. Later that night, Governor José Antonio Viscarra and Lieutenant Colonel José Antonio Arze led a parade through the streets accompanied by a musical troupe, singing songs "appropriate to the occasion." Shouts of "*viva el emperador*" punctuated the cold December night until two in the morning.

The celebration continued before sunrise the following day, December 11, with artillery salvos and a parade through the streets. At nine in the morning, a mass was sung at the parish church and a patriotic sermon delivered by the pastor of Santa Cruz de la Cañada, Francisco Rada. At four in the afternoon, the Imperial Standard was brought out from the parish church in a noble procession led by a young boy dressed as an angel. The boy held a sword in his hand and was followed by a second boy dressed in black, representing Padre Miguel Hidalgo. Don Pedro Armendaris, the *Alférez Publico* (public or civil standard bearer), followed on horseback carrying the "Imperial Standard" of the Emperor. Trailing Armendaris were José Francisco Baca, *primer alcalde* of Santa Fe, and local officers Juan Vigil, Agapito Alva, and Santiago Abreu.

The procession of dignitaries was followed by a young girl representing Liberty seated in an elaborately adorned cart. Two women, one representing North America and the other South America, stood at her side, both connected to Liberty by a sash.

Figure 3. Portrait of Agustín de Iturbide by Primitivo Miranda, 1865. Museo Nacional de Historia, Mexico City.

Slightly above and behind Liberty was a bust of the emperor with a young girl representing Justice holding a silver crown in both hands, as if crowning the emperor. At the rear marched musicians and the alférez, Felipe Griego, with an escort of forty soldiers in column and sixteen elaborately dressed young boys and girls in two files, each wearing a sash of ribbon on which was written "*viva el Emperador*." Behind them followed two troupes of matachines, one composed of children and another of adult men. Seven groups from the various pueblos danced along the route of the procession.

The parade continued to the plaza, where Armendaris set the Imperial Standard on a platform erected near the entrance to the corridor of the palace facing the plaza. As soon as Armendaris stepped down from the platform, the public celebration began as the Pueblo Indians and matachines danced and table games were opened.

That night, a theatre was set up on the plaza and an opera presented that featured three principal characters. Don José María Baca, secretary of the ayuntamiento, portrayed the King of Spain, the alférez Felipe Griego, the king's Minister of State, and Santiago Abreu, the Mexican ambassador. A dance followed at the governor's residence, "in which gentlemen and ladies offered toasts in the name of the emperor, and every song and shout was directed to his honor."

The following day, December 12, the governor and local officials took an oath of allegiance to "Dn. Agustín as First Mexican Emperor" at an altar that was erected next to the platform on which the Imperial Standard had been placed the previous day. When these ceremonies concluded, dances and other festivities continued until seven that night when a colloquy to Our Lady of Guadalupe was presented (it was, after all, December 12). This was followed by a "discourse between Moors and Christians" and a presentation by the children's matachines. A dance followed at the house of don Juan Pino. The following day, another procession was held, followed by patriotic speeches, music, and a comedy prepared by don Domingo Fernandes. An evening dance held at the house of don Atanacio Bolivar concluded the festivities.

Within three months of this celebration, New Mexico received communications from Mexico advising that Iturbide had been deposed as emperor. His short-lived reign as Emperor of Mexico, however, left a fascinating record of three days of enthusiastic celebration that marked one of New Mexico's first documented observations of Mexican independence from Spain.

Governor Armijo Orders Road Repairs, 1827

In a tersely worded letter dated June 5, 1827, less than a month after he had taken the oath of office for his first term as governor, Manuel Armijo scolded the alcaldes of the middle Rio Grande Valley jurisdictions of Alameda, Sandia, Cochiti, and Albuquerque. He bluntly noted that when he had traveled between the capital in Santa Fe and his home in the villa of Albuquerque, he found the road and the acequias and *desagues* (irrigation ditches and drainage areas) in desperate need of repairs. He reminded these local officials that it was their responsibility and that of the ayuntamientos to maintain the roads and ensure the safety and convenience of travelers.

Governor Armijo warned that he planned to return to Santa Fe the following week and expected to find the roads, bridges, acequias, and their desagues "perfectly repaired." He also warned local officials that if there was the slightest delay in carrying out the orders, they would be held personally responsible for any damages suffered by travelers, and threatened to fine them whatever amount he found convenient if his coach suffered a breakdown when he returned to the capital because the roads had not been repaired.

The tone of the order suggests Governor Armijo was in a bad mood. Less than a month earlier he had begun what would be his first of three terms as governor when he took the oath of office on May 20, 1827 (technically he was the *gefe politico*, or political chief, but the term governor is utilized for convenience). The following day, he began his term of office without a staff or place to live. On May 21, Francisco Pérez Serrano resigned from the important post of secretary to the governor because of the persistent insecurity of funding for the position's salary. It had apparently been standard practice for the governor to assume personal responsibility for the salary of his secretary because the treasury usually lacked the funds to pay them and Pérez Serrano resigned because Armijo refused to make that guarantee. Armijo then appointed Santiago Abreu as his secretary and Rafael Sarracino as his scribe. Abreu and Sarracino took the positions with the understanding that Armijo would not be personally responsible for paying them.

If Governor Armijo was in a bad mood, however, it may have been because, as a resident of the villa of Albuquerque, he did not have a home in Santa Fe and within two days of when he took the oath of office, he found out that he did not have a place to stay in the capital. In the weeks that followed, he discovered that access to the Palace of the Governors—the place we automatically assume served as a home and office for Spanish- and Mexican-era governors—did not fall automatically to governors-select. At least not in this instance.

Two days after he took the oath of office, Armijo wrote his predecessor, former governor Antonio Narbona, and suggested it was "indecorous" that the newly appointed head of government did not have an official residence. He asked Narbona, who retained the position of *comandante principal* (military commander of the presidio garrison), to either vacate the palace or produce documents that proved occupancy of the palace was the purview of the comandante principal. Narbona responded quickly, noting that the palace complex was constructed by and for the military and suggested Armijo appeal to the president of the republic if he disagreed. The issue was even taken up in a special, closed session of the diputación on May 25, but their resolution, while supportive of the governor, did not seem to make a very strong case for Armijo's right to possess the palace.

In late June, more than a month after he took the oath of office, Armijo was still indignant about his housing situation. He was renting a room in a private home, living with the owner's wife and family, and was unable to bring his own wife to Santa Fe. His secretary had only a small, cramped room to work in and had no access to the archives because they were located in the *palacio*. In another letter dated July 11, Armijo claimed the situation had worsened because the American commercial caravan was due to arrive any day and the owner of the house where he was living also provided rooms and meals to the Americans, making his situation more untenable and undignified.

It is not clear at what point Governor Armijo was able to move into the palace. On July 24, 1827, Narbona officially turned over military command of the presidio garrison to Captain José Caballero and the August muster of the garrison shows that the *cabo* (corporal) Andres Ortega and eight soldiers were escorting Narbona on his way to Mexico. There is no indication that the occupancy issue continued under Caballero, so Governor Armijo may have taken up residence at the palacio in late July or early August.

Manuel Armijo's first term as governor lasted less than two years. On March 21, 1829, José Antonio Chaves, senior member of the diputación took the oath of office as the new gefe politico, but there is no indication as to whether he took up residency at the Palace of the Governors at that time.

Orderly Succession to Office

One of the fascinating elements of how governments functioned during the Spanish and Mexican periods is how one governor assumed office from another when a new governor was appointed. It may be surprising to some that these successions were typically carried out in a very formal and orderly manner (the issue of Governor Armijo being unable to take possession of the Palace of the Governors in 1827 notwithstanding). This process is nowhere better documented than the surviving records of the late Mexican period.

During New Mexico's Mexican period there was no office of lieutenant governor. Succession to office in the event of a governor's death, illness, or absence from the villa of Santa Fe fell to the *primer vocal*, the most senior member of the legislative council. When the governor left Santa Fe on official or personal business even for a few days, he had to notify the council and formally turn over civil authority to whoever held that position.

The process of succession for a governor who was leaving office unfolds beautifully in the weeks following Manuel Armijo's resignation from his second term of office on December 10, 1843. A month later, on January 9, 1844, Armijo, citing issues with his health, notified the Department Assembly that he was leaving. During the one and a half years from January 1844, when Manuel Armijo resigned from his second term of governor, to when he was appointed to his third and last term in July 1845, four other men held the office in the interim—Mariano Chaves y Castillo (January to April 1844), Felipe Sena (April 1844), Mariano Martínez (April 1844–April 1845), and José Chaves (April–July 1845).

On January 31, 1844, Mariano Chaves y Castillo, as primer vocal of the Department Assembly, assumed *mando del gobierno* (command of the government) and was sworn in as interim governor at the Palace of the Governors. Meanwhile, the assembly prepared a list of five nominees for the governorship, which was sent to the supreme government in Mexico. The full list is not in our archives, but indications are, Mariano Martínez was at the top of the list. On February 12, 1844, Martínez wrote to the assembly, advising them he had heard (there must have been "leaks" in the old days too) that his name had been placed at the top of the list of nominees for governor, thanking the assembly for the honor, and assuring them that if appointed he would do his best to serve the territory.

Over the next month, the nominations made their way through the Mexican hierarchy and on about March 30, 1844, the decision was made to appoint Mariano Martínez as governor of New Mexico. The decision was immediately forwarded to the Ministerio de Guerra y Marina (Ministry of War and Navy) in Mexico City, where the appointment was confirmed and Martínez notified in a letter dated April 5, 1844.

Meanwhile, back in New Mexico, interim governor Mariano Chaves y Castillo became ill and informed the assembly that he could no longer serve in the office. On April 12, 1844, unaware that Mariano Martínez had already been appointed by the government in Mexico, the assembly asked Manuel Armijo to return to Santa Fe and resume command of the government until his replacement was named. Armijo's response is not on record, but he must have refused the honor because Felipe Sena, as the senior council member, assumed the functions of governor that same day.

News of Mariano Martínez's appointment as governor arrived in Santa Fe on April 29, 1844. That day, the assembly and Martínez simultaneously advised each other that they had received notice of the appointment and after some discussion, set May 15 as the date for his inauguration to office. Martínez served as governor for almost exactly one year. The correspondence logs for his term of office are a wonderful source of information for anyone wishing to refute the long-held and erroneous notion that New Mexico was isolated, cut off from the government in Mexico and the world in general. His records show a regular flow of correspondence received from all parts of Mexico. Letters from officials in Yucatán, Chiapas, Tamaulipas, Sinaloa, San Luis Potosí, Nuevo León, Morelia, Aguascalientes, Puebla, Guanajuato, Zacatecas, Durango and Chihuahua kept New Mexico informed of local events, changes in government, and appointments to office. Newly appointed governors in New Mexico often received letters of congratulations and well wishes from various Mexican states and cities, indicating that news of what was happening in New Mexico was widely distributed to other parts of the Mexican Republic.

On April 14, 1845, Governor Martínez received orders from the superior government in Mexico that he was to hand over civil government to the *vocal aquien corresponda* (the assembly member to whom it corresponds), and on April 20, 1845, José Chaves, as the primer vocal of the Department Assembly received orders to present himself at the capital as soon as possible so that he could assume the position of interim governor, due to Martínez's resignation. It is not clear if Chaves was sworn into office on April 30 or May 1, but the later date is when Martínez notified his superiors in Mexico and the local prefects that he had turned over command of the civil government of New Mexico to Chaves. That same day, Martínez delivered a "farewell address," noting that he did not presume to have solved all the region's problems during his short tenure as governor, but did take credit for negotiations that he felt had improved relations with the Navajos and Utes and emphasized his efforts to conciliate differences between the territory's political factions.

For the next several days, there was a flurry of correspondence in which interim governor Chaves notified officials in Mexico and locally that he had assumed the governorship, and there was acknowledgment of the same by these officers. But Chaves was only the interim governor, and on May 13, the assembly met in an "extraordinary session" to prepare a *quintero de gobernador,* a list of five names they deemed qualified to be considered as nominees for governor. The first name listed was Manuel Armijo, followed by Mariano Chaves (who died that week), Juan Perea, Antonio Ortiz, and Vicente Martínez. There is no record of when this list of nominees was submitted to the superior government in Mexico, but it must have been quite soon after it was prepared because within days of May 13, the Department Assembly informed officials in Mexico that Mariano Chaves had died and should be removed from the list.

There is no indication in our Mexican-era archives of the form in which this list of nominees was submitted. It is likely that a simple list of names would not suffice for officials in Mexico to consider, so we may wonder if the list included biographical information or resumes of the nominees. Certainly Manuel Armijo's name and qualifications would have been well known since he had already served two terms as governor, but it would be interesting to see if the assembly listed the qualifications they felt each of the five nominees had.

Regardless, on July 24, 1845, the Ministerio de Relaciones Exteriores, Guerra y Justicia (Ministry of Foreign Relations, War and Justice) advised interim governor José Chaves that the president had appointed Manuel Armijo to his third term as governor and ordered he be placed in possession of the office. It is not clear when Armijo received notice of his appointment or why there was a four-month delay in his taking office. Finally, on November 14, 1845, Chaves acknowledged a letter from Armijo advising he was on his way to Santa Fe (presumably from his home in Albuquerque) and expected to arrive at the capital the following afternoon, November 15. Chaves indicated that he was making plans to meet Armijo at the outskirts of the city and asked the military commander to prepare "a decorous entrance" for the new governor. Details of what constituted this "decorous entrance" are missing but it likely included an escort of troops into the city, the firing of cannons, and the ringing of church bells.

Chaves officially turned over the command of New Mexico's civil government to Manuel Armijo on November 16, 1845. That day, Chaves sent out letters to various officials in New Mexico advising that at 10:00 a.m. that morning, the "General Don Manuel Armijo" had taken possession of the government and that he (Chaves) had separated from the position.

That same day, Armijo prepared several letters informing officials in Mexico and the local prefects that he had taken possession of the office. It is unlikely that Armijo had any idea he would be New Mexico's last Mexican-era governor. Two weeks after Armijo was sworn into his third term as governor, the United States admitted the nascent Republic of Texas into the Union and the dark clouds of war between the United States and Mexico soon loomed large over New Mexico. A mere nine months after he took his final oath of office, Manuel Armijo would face the fateful decision of what to do about the approaching American Army of the West under General Stephen Watts Kearny.

The Forced Loan of 1829

One of the persistent problems New Mexico experienced during its Mexican period (1821–1846) was the province's inability to raise enough revenue to adequately support its military garrison and pay its civilian employees. On several occasions when the government needed extra revenue to meet unexpected or emergency situations, they imposed what were called "forced loans" in which the territory's citizens were assigned to contribute specific amounts in the guise of a loan that may or may not be repaid in the future.

One of the best documented loans of this type begins with a July 6, 1829, order from the gefe politico, José Antonio Chaves, in which he tasked the alcaldes to gather the individuals in their jurisdiction who had assets of property or cash valued at more than 1,000 pesos and required each individual to prepare a sworn statement as to "every class of assets and income derived from these." These sworn statements were to be submitted to the governor so he could develop a list of individuals among whom he could assign the 18,000-peso assessment of the forced loan.

Twenty-seven of these sworn statements have survived, most from the southern New Mexico jurisdictions. These consist of ten individuals from the jurisdiction of Albuquerque: Manuel Armijo, Gregorio Ortiz, Cristobal Pacheco, Lucas Armijo, Francisco Sabedra, Feliz García, Julian Armijo, Abel Ylisarri, Andres Ortega, and Rosalía Mestas, the only woman on the list; eight from Santa Fe: Clemente Esquibel, Juan Rafael Ortiz, Ygnacio Baca, José Francisco Baca, Diego Montoya, Antonio Ortiz, José Guadalupe Romero, and Pablo Montoya; Bartolomé Baca and

Jacinto Sánchez from Tomé; Joaquín Alarid from Peralta; Vicente Otero from Valencia; Juan Antonio Cabesa de Baca from Peña Blanca; Antonio Reyes from Cochiti; and Pascual Guacamalla and Toribio Romero from Puesto de Laguna.

Among the extant sworn statements, two of the men with the most assets included former governor Bartolomé Baca, whose listed assets included 8,000 sheep, 214 cattle, 80 horses, and 25 tame mules. He estimated his resources produced an income of 1,500 pesos a year. Manuel Armijo's sworn statement lists his house of residence and property in the villa of Albuquerque, land at Carnuel, and nearly 10,000 sheep and numerous other livestock. Armijo estimated his property produced 100 fanegas (a unit of measurement of approximately two and a half bushels) of corn, fifty of wheat, six of beans and 100 *ristras* (strings) of chile, but does not include a value of his assets or his income. Certainly, Baca and Armijo, both prominent in the economic and political affairs of New Mexico and who, between them, served a total of four terms as governor, would easily qualify for inclusion on any list of the wealthiest people in New Mexico at that point in history.

Subsequent reports, however, show that New Mexican officials had trouble collecting the 18,000-peso assessment, and on October of 1829, the diputación, presumably using the lists provided by the alcaldes, compiled a list of specific amounts it was assigning to each jurisdiction:

For the *rio arriba*:

Santa Fe: 1,200 pesos

Taos: 1,400 pesos

Abiquiú: 1,000 pesos
Santa Cruz de la Cañada: 750 pesos
San Juan: 500 pesos
San Miguel del Bado: 350 pesos

For the *rio abajo*:
Cochiti: 350 pesos
Xemes: 200 pesos
Sandia: 700 pesos
Albuquerque: 1,200 pesos
Ysleta: 8,000 pesos
Tomé: 1,200 pesos
Sabinal: 200 pesos
Socorro: 100 pesos
Laguna: 250 pesos

At least two lists have survived that show how the 1829 loan amounts were assigned to individuals within specific jurisdictions. The list for Abiquiú has twenty-seven names on it, with several of those at the top of the list being well-known men of means, including Pedro Ygnacio Gallegos and Manuel Martines. The first seven individuals on the list for Abiquiú were assigned ninety pesos each for a total of 630 pesos. The balance of the 1,000 pesos assessed on Abiquiú was distributed among the next twenty people in decreasing amounts, varying from forty to ten pesos, with the last four names donating between five and three pesos each for a total of 1,000 pesos. The other surviving list, from the jurisdiction of Jemez, took a different tack. They distributed its assignment of 200 pesos among eighty-seven individuals. Most are listed with a one-peso contribution and several with as little as four reales (1/2 peso). The largest assigned contribution from Jemez was two pesos by Ygnacio Vigil.

A Peace Conference with the Comanches, 1829

On July 14, 1829, gefe politico José Antonio Chaves informed comandante principal Juan José Arocha that twelve Comanches led by the chief (*capitán*) Samporallena had come to Santa Fe to invite them to "go to the desert" at Bosque Redondo to discuss issues related to a peace treaty the Comanches had made (or were considering) with Texas.

The next several days were spent planning for the meeting and requesting funds from revenue officials to purchase provisions for the fifty presidio troops who were to accompany the expedition and for unspecified gifts for the Comanches. The subsequent expedition took nearly two weeks and is described in a nicely detailed diary kept by Governor Chaves. According to the diary, the expedition consisted of the fifty presidio soldiers and seventy-five citizens who went along to trade with the Comanches. A separate report and diary were remitted by the military commander Arocha, but it is not utilized for this article.

The following is a summary of the daily events listed in the Chaves diary. The details are included here for readers who may be familiar with the place names noted in the diary and may want to map the route taken from Santa Fe to Bosque Redondo. Of special interest to this author was the daily notation that the expedition stopped at an unspecified hour (likely late morning or early afternoon) for a siesta, or rest, which must have been important because the diary made a point to note the few times they did not stop:

> July 19: Began the march, took siesta (*sestie*) at Peñas Negras, and spent the night at the Sienega de Pecos. That night Chaves was informed that the Comanche captain (*capitancillo*) named Lamparrallena and fourteen Comanches who accompanied him had not eaten all day, so an ox was purchased and butchered to feed them.
>
> July 20: Left the Sienega de Pecos, stopped for siesta at the Palo Flechado, and spent the night at Bado, where they purchased another ox to feed the Comanches.
>
> July 21: After leaving Bado, they took siesta at Cañoncito de Peña and proceeded to Anton Chico for the night.
>
> July 22: From Anton Chico, they made siesta at Cañon Blanco, where Chaves noted the desert begins (*aqui comiensa el desierto*). From there the Comanche captain Lamparrallena, eight of his warriors, and two soldiers went ahead to locate the Comanche camp and ask them to meet the expedition at la Cañada de Juan de Dios, then made camp for the night at the Valle de Guadalupe.
>
> July 23: From the Valle de Guadalupe they proceeded to Agua Negra without stopping for siesta.

July 24: Proceeding from Agua Negra, they made siesta at the Cañada de Juan de Dios, where one of the soldiers who had gone ahead with the Comanches returned to advise Chaves that the son of Comanche general Parnaquivisti was ill, so they would instead wait for the expedition at Bosque Redondo. They made camp for the night at the Sabino Quemado, located in the Cañada de Juan de Dios.

July 25: The chaplain celebrated Mass before leaving the Sabino Quemado, taking siesta at the Alamogordo. That afternoon they were met by General Parnaquivisti, his chiefs (*sus capitanes*), and more than one hundred warriors, and the expedition proceeded to the Bosque Redondo, where they made camp.

July 26: Being Sunday, the chaplain celebrated Mass. At 9:00 a.m. Chaves, Arocha, their secretary, militia officers, and several citizens met with Parnaquivisti and others of his tribe in a large campaign tent to discuss the purpose of the meeting—a letter from Mexican vice president Anastasio Bustamante that sought Comanche assurances that they would desist from raiding the Eastern States of Tejas, Coahuila, and Chihuahua. The Cománches agreed to caution their young men from such foolishness (*tontería*) and would go to Bexar to present Lieutenant Colonel Francisco Ruiz with a document prepared by Chaves and Arocha formalizing their agreement. The Comanches were then presented with a number of gifts, which included tobacco, panocha, mirrors, sarapes, scissors, and knives.

July 27: At Bosque Redondo, at eight in the morning, Chaves and Arocha met with Parnaquivisti and his principal captain, Namallape, and handed them the document they were to take to Bexar. At three that afternoon they broke camp and traveled to Alamogordo, where they spent the night.

July 28–30: From Alamogordo they retraced their return route through la Cañada de Juan de Dios, Agua Negra, Valle de Guadalupe, Cañon Blanco, Puertecito, and Bado. At Bado they were informed of a man who had been wounded by raiders at the Cañada de Felipe Sanches and a squad of soldiers and several volunteer citizens under command of Capitan José Caballero were sent to pursue the raiders and if possible, catch and punish them.

July 31–August 1: The remaining expedition departed Bado and returned to Santa Fe. Governor Chaves noted the distance from Bosque Redondo to Santa Fe was seventy-eight leagues (approximately 180 miles. The modern official map mileage indicates it is 152 miles from Santa Fe to Fort Sumner via modern highways) from the capital in Santa Fe to Bosque Redondo.

Proposal for New Mexico Statehood, 1831

On March 9, 1831, Juan Estévan Pino, Juan Felipe Ortiz, and José Francisco Baca submitted a proposal to gefe politico José Antonio Chaves. The ayuntamientos of the territory, they elegantly noted, "lift[ed] their voices, for the first time, to the supreme legislative body of the federation, imploring the remedy they seek to overcome the maladies they experience" and urged Chaves to join them in an effort to have New Mexico admitted as a state in the Mexican Republic. They suggested New Mexico could be known as the "Estado de Hidalgo" and cited the territory's "most ardent desire" to achieve the status of a "free and sovereign state."

The petitioners asked Governor Chaves to circulate the proposal to the ayuntamientos of the territory for their consideration and support and laid out an interesting perspective on how necessary statehood was to correct the current status of the administrative, especially the judicial system in New Mexico. The proposal emphasized that civil and criminal cases were seldom brought to a conclusion because appeals had to be made via the long and costly process of sending them to Mexico for review because local judicial officials were generally ignorant of the law. Too often, suspects and convicted prisoners had to be placed in jail for prolonged periods because appeals took so long, and under the Spanish- and Mexican-era judicial system, New Mexico had few, if any, secure jails. Criminals often avoided punishment by escaping, and in the words of the petitioners, made a mockery of the judicial system.

The petition includes an optimistic budget document listing projected revenues and expenses for the new state. They included what they felt would be needed to cover the operations of legislative, executive, and judicial branches, noting that New Mexico derived most of its revenue from the tariffs imposed on imports from the annual commercial caravans. The authors speculated that even if the revenues and expenses of the proposed state budget only "broke even," it would provide for everything the new state of Hidalgo required to function effectively.

Between March 13 and 31, 1831, the proposal made its way to the ayuntamientos, beginning with the villa of Santa Fe and continued to Sandia, Belen, Tomé, Sabinal, San Miguel de Socorro, Laguna, Jémez, San Geronimo de Taos, and the villa de Albuquerque. On April 12 and 13, the proposal was presented to the diputación, which, after a long and heated debate, turned down the proposal by a four-to-one vote. On April 20, the governor's secretary informed the petition's authors of Chaves's personal opposition to the proposal as well as other unspecified "general dissent" that made the timing "inconvenient." The proposal was set aside and archived until circumstances allowed for its revival. That same day, Ramón Abreu, the diputación secretary, acknowledged the governor's notice that he had set aside the proposal and lauded Pino, Ortiz, and Baca, the proposal's authors, for their patriotism and desire to "elevate this Territory as a sovereign and independent state." While individuals at the highest echelons of government rejected the statehood proposal, it seems clear that elements of New Mexican society felt strongly that being an integral part of the larger Mexican federation was important for the advancement of the territory.

In addition to the importance these petitioners placed on establishing New Mexico as an independent state in the Mexican Republic, the accompanying statements of support from the ayuntamientos provide us with a rare list of the individuals who held local office in most of the ayuntamientos throughout the territory. The following are the names and office each signatory held at the listed municipalities. Note that names are spelled as they are in the document:

Santa Fe (March 13)

Pablo Montoya, Alcalde
Cristobal Torres, Regidor (municipal council member)
Francisco Archiveque, Regidor
Domingo Jimenes [Illegible], Secretario

Sandia (March 13)

José Martínez, Alcalde
Antonio Lusero, Regidor
Jesus Lusero, Regidor
Jose Tenorio, Secretario

Villa of Albuquerque (March 14)

Ambrosio Armijo, Alcalde
Juan Montoya, Regidor
Feliz García, Regidor
Antonio N. Ruiz (?), Secretario

Tomé (March 15)

Juan Baca Chaves, Presidente (as Alcalde)
Nereo Antonio Montolla, Regidor
Antonio Barela, Regidor
Miguel de Olona, Regidor

Belen (March 16)

Juan Cruz Baca, Alcalde
Diego Armijo, Regidor
Pablo Baca, Regidor
Domingo Castillo, Secretario

Sabinal (March 17)

Román Torres, Alcalde
Miguel Beita, Regidor
Antonio José Apodaca, Regidor
Manuel Ballejos, Secretario

San Miguel del Socorro (March 18)

José Campos Redondo, Alcalde
Diego Antonio Sanches, Sindico
Mariano Ulibarri, Regidor
Rafael Arroyos, Secretario

Laguna (March 23)

Juan Bautista Romero, Alcalde
Lorenzo Romero, Regidor
Antonio Torres, Regidor
Eusebio Aragón, Secretario

Xemes (March 25)

Manuel Montoya, Alcalde
Juan Montoya, Regidor
Mateo Armenta, Sindico
Tomás Manuel Montoya, Secretario

San Geronimo de Taos (March 31)

Juan Antonio Aragón, Presidente
Santiago Martínez, Regidor
José Tomás Romero (?), Regidor
Antonio Ortiz, Secretario

The *Muralla*—Living Quarters for the Troops

One of the persistent and perplexing questions about our venerable Palace of the Governors is that we know very little about what it looked like through the centuries. We know there has been a government complex that is often referred to as the casas reales around the plaza since the seventeenth century. While we do not know what these buildings may have looked like when originally constructed after the villa of Santa Fe was established in 1610, we know they underwent significant changes during the Pueblo occupation in 1680 and following the reconquista by Diego de Vargas in the late seventeenth century. There is even strong evidence that a portion of the palace had a second story in the early eighteenth century.

One extant map of the villa of Santa Fe, drawn by Joseph de Urrutia in 1768, shows a "Casa del Gobernador" on the north side of the plaza, where the palace is located today. There are also two detailed drawings of the new *quartel,* a massive construction project that was completed in 1790–1791 to provide consolidated housing units for the presidio troops. The exterior walls of this new quartel, which extended north from the plaza possibly as far as where the federal courthouse and post office are located today, came to be known as the *muralla,* a term normally used to describe the ramparts of a fortified structure.

Figure 4. (*opposite*)"Plano de el Presidio de Santa Fe," 1791. Archivo General de la Nación. Provincias Internas de Nuevo Mexico, 1763–1772 (Tomo 161). The present-day Palace of the Governors is designated as D and E in the illustration.

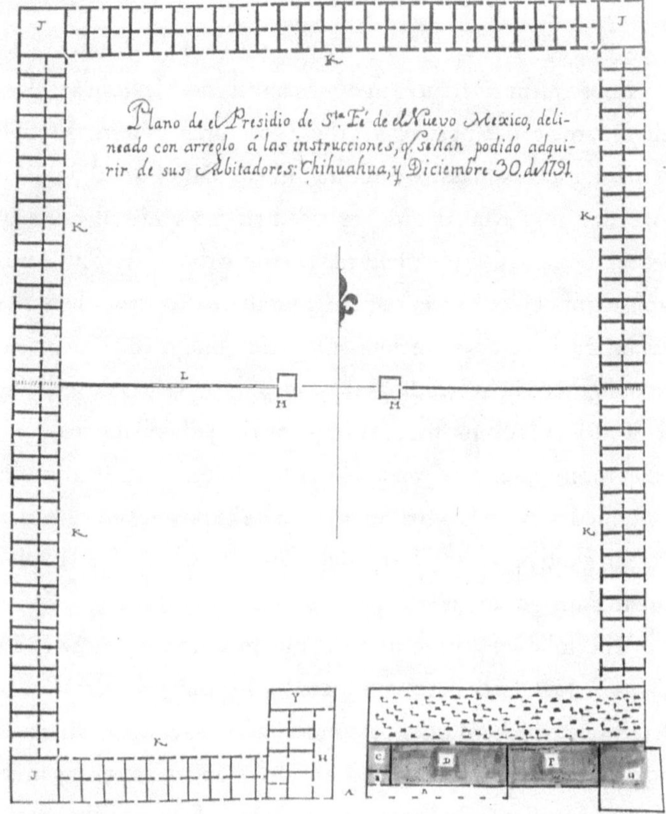

Explicación (Key)

A. Entrada al presidio (entrance to presidio)
B. Cuerpo de guardia (guardhouse)
C. Carcel (jail)
D. Casa para el gobernador (house for the governor)
E. Su huerta (his garden)
F. Abilitación (commissary)
G. Baluarte (bulwark)
H. Entrada a las casas (entrance to the houses)
Y. Casa para aloxamiento (visitors' quarters)
J. Casas para los sargentos (sergeants' houses)
K. Idem para la tropa con sus repectivos corrales (same for the troops and their respective corrales)
L. Conductas de agua (water passages, acequias)
M. Labaderos (washstands)

Subsequent references in our Spanish and Mexican archives tell us of the constant struggles these governments went through to maintain this massive building. In late fall of 1810, interim governor José Manrrique reported that torrential rains in September and October had caused more than fifty-four varas (approximately 150 feet) of the muralla to collapse. It is not certain if any repairs were done at that time but in 1825, an inventory of government buildings described the palacio as consisting of twenty-six rooms, three rooms for the jail (calabozos), and a flag room (*quarto de vanderas*). It also noted that the muralla contained 115 rooms (or housing units), sixty-seven of which were in good order, and forty-eight of which were uninhabitable due to damages incurred by heavy rains and humidity.

The following year, in a document dated April 6, 1826, Captain José Caballero conducted a formal investigation to determine which military personnel had taken doors, windows, vigas, and boards (*tabletas*) from the uninhabitable housing units of the muralla. Caballero's report lists 115 units, numbered sequentially from 1 through 115. Thirty-seven are shown as *despobladas* (abandoned), and list what was missing from each, and who took the missing items. Unit number 1, for example, shows it to be assigned to Sergeant José Silba, but was abandoned and missing its windows and doors. It was not known who took them. Likewise, units 3 and 4 were abandoned and without windows, which were taken by Santiago Armijo and José Salaises. It should be noted that Salaises and Armijo are shown living in other units, numbers 5 and 40, respectively, so it is possible that these individuals used the windows and doors taken from units 3 and 4 to make repairs to their own housing unit or residence. This may also have been the case in unit number 66, which is shown as "complete" and inhabited by the *invalido* (retired soldier) Martín Gallego. Gallego lived adjacent to unit 67, which was missing windows, doors, and four vigas, all of which were "in the house of Martín Gallego."

When the names on this list are compared to the April 1826 muster of the presidio company, most of the 105 officers and men of the company, including Captain José Caballero in unit 109, lived in units assigned to them within the muralla. However, some soldiers apparently lived "off campus" and possibly used items from the muralla to repair their private homes or quarters. Unit ninety-seven, for example, is listed as abandoned, and it is stated that Sergeant Manuel Baca took the doors, windows, vigas, and boards. However, Baca, who is listed in the April 1826 muster, is not shown as residing in any of the muralla units.

Thirty-seven units along the muralla are listed as abandoned or simply as vacant, even though someone was assigned to some of them. It may be significant that there is a section of seven units, numbers ninety-one through ninety-seven, of which only one was occupied. There is no indication what size any of the 115 units were, but one can wonder if this section constituted the 150 feet of muralla destroyed by the rains of 1810 that never underwent any repairs or reconstruction. No illustrations of the quartel for the Mexican period have been found but the 1846 Gilmore map of Santa Fe labels the structures behind the Palace of the Governors as the "Old Military Barracks," while the Hughes map of the same year labels them as the "Quartel." Both show apparent gaps in the muralla.

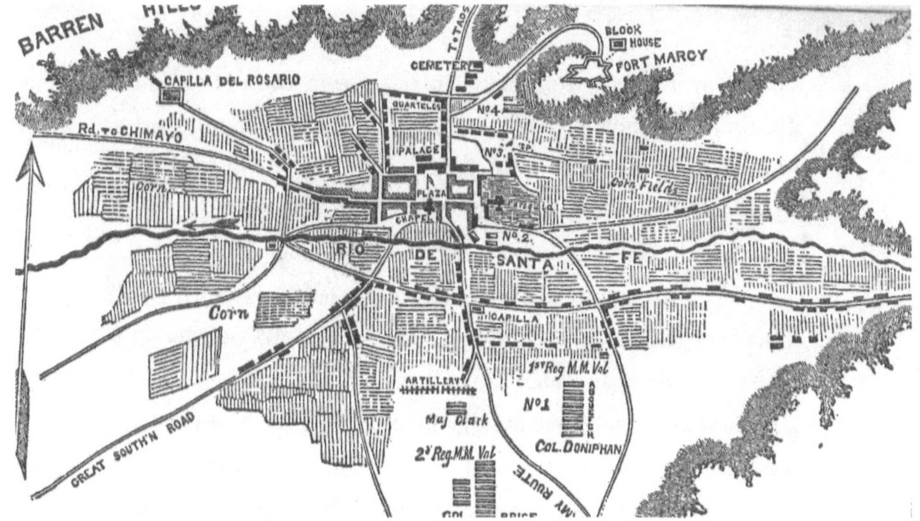

Figure 5. The John Taylor Hughes 1846 "Plan of Santa Fe and its Environs" shows gaps along the "*quarteles*" possibly reflecting the deteriorating condition of the *muralla*. John Taylor Hughes, *Doniphan's Expedition* (Texas A & M University Press, 1997), 49.

Repairing the *Casas Reales*, 1832

In the previous chapter we reviewed several occasions when Spanish- and Mexican-era officials authorized and made repairs to the complex of buildings known as the casas reales that eventually resulted in the new quartel, the military barracks and government buildings of which today's Palace of the Governors was a part. During his term as governor, Juan Bautista de Anza actually proposed to move the military garrison out of the villa of Santa Fe and relocate it to a site along the middle Rio Grande Valley between the pueblos of Cochiti and Santo Domingo.

Although Anza's plans were thwarted, his successor, Governor Fernando de la Concha, implemented a massive construction project that reshaped the entire layout of the capital city that we now consider downtown. His plans called for construction of new buildings that consolidated housing for the presidio troops and their families at a site north of the plaza area.

Preparations for construction of the new quartel probably began in the spring of 1788. By January 1789, Governor Concha reported that lumber had been cut and stacked, and straw and other materials gathered, and that adobes were being made and stacked that following spring. The scale of the project may be reflected by one report that noted that a devastating downpour destroyed nearly eighty thousand adobes. When the project was completed by late 1790 or early 1791, ninety-eight new residential units were completed and soon inhabited by presidio soldiers and their families. Of the building constructed more than two hundred years ago, only that part we know as the Palace of the Governors exists today. Of special interest in this process is a March 27, 1789, *bando*, or order, by Governor Concha that instructed the alcaldes of surrounding communities to prepare lists of men aged sixteen through fifty who would be eligible to work on construction of the new building. Unfortunately, there are no surviving lists of those who reported to work on the project. It would be extraordinarily interesting for New Mexicans to see such lists and be able to identify ancestors who helped to construct the new quartel for the presidio of Santa Fe.

However, by the 1820s, documents in our Mexican Archives of New Mexico make it clear that the presidio compound had deteriorated badly because of poor construction or neglect and was in frequent need of repairs. One 1832 report suggested that the governor's house (the report does not call it the Palace of the Governors) was in danger of collapsing, and that three hundred pesos were budgeted for the most urgent repairs. The records do not show how the entire budget was expended, but one financial document has survived that provides details of some much-needed repairs done on a portion of the presidio complex. It even lists the names of several individuals, the specific work they did, and how much they were paid. The heading of this document shows that each individual was paid three reales (⅜ of a peso) for each day worked. While some of the men were paid in cash, most were paid in rations, measured in almudes of corn or wheat, with the value of each measure placed at three reales—the equivalent of one day's wages.

An 1832 report from the presidio company accounting records shows repairs done on the *guardia* (guard house), *tienda* (quartermaster store), and *granero* (granary) in late June 1832. Miguel Gonzales, José María Montoya, and Manuel Ortis were each paid between six pesos and three pesos in cash for the days they worked, while Miguel Martín, José Antonio Ortiz, Santiago Langel, and Juan José Antonio Ortiz were paid in rations of one almud of corn at the equivalent rate of three reales a day. There is no indication as to what specific work any of these men did.

Several other tasks were listed without the workers being identified. Five laborers (peones) for tamping or leveling (*apretilando*) the floors, a mason and two peones to install the door to the guardia, and two peones to plaster or whitewash (*encalar*) the guardia.

The following were identified by name and what they were paid for the specific work they did. Ramon Corís was paid six almudes of grain for providing eight almudes of gypsum (yeso) used to whitewash the guardia. Carpenter Matías Sena was paid more than twenty pesos in cash and rations to build seventeen *canales* (drain channels) for the guardia and tienda at two reales each. Sena also built a door for the guardia and provided three pounds of iron (possibly for the hinges of the door). José Rivera was paid one and a half fanegas of grain (approximately four bushels) to place hinges (*engosnar*) on the door and to prepare two logs (*palos*) for the porch of the guardia. Finally, Joaquín Martín was paid nearly two pesos in grain for some adobes, to prime (*blanciar*) the new guardia door and paint it blue, plus two pesos cash for two ounces of tint (*añil*) to make the paint. In total, slightly more than fifty-one pesos was expended for the repairs.

Governor Albino Pérez and the Revolt of 1837

On Thursday, June 14, 2007, a fascinating ceremony was held in the courtyard of the Palace of the Governors. That day, the Daughters of the American Revolution (DAR) rededicated and officially donated a stone memorial to the Museum of New Mexico. On this same day in 1901, the DAR had installed this memorial along the road in Agua Fria to commemorate the site where Governor Albino Pérez was assassinated on the night of August 8, 1837.

Albino Pérez assumed the office of governor on May 23, 1835. Pérez came to New Mexico during a period of great change and uncertainty. He had arrived as an outsider and indications are, he was looked upon with suspicion and distrust. He also had the unenviable task of instituting the new Mexican constitution of 1836. The new constitution made New Mexico a department of the republic and established a system of government that replaced the centuries-old system of alcaldes. The new constitution also suspended the ayuntamientos and replaced the traditional diputación with a departmental junta.

Pérez was also tasked with imposing something that New Mexico had never experienced—a direct tax. We do not know the specifics of how this taxation was to be implemented but such a tax was opposed by most New Mexicans. For centuries, the citizens of New Mexico had borne the expense—in money, time, and lives—of defending the frontier against the many tribes that raided the villages and pueblos of the territory. In recognition of this service, New Mexico was regularly granted exemptions from direct taxes.

In the midst of all this were the Americans. By 1835 trade along the Santa Fe Trail was well established. The tariffs and taxes imposed on the American traders and merchants constituted virtually all the revenue the government relied on to support the presidio troops and pay salaries. The Americans despised the taxes and had little respect for the Mexican government and its laws.

The situation in New Mexico came to a boil in the summer of 1837: the province was besieged by enemies from all sides; the central government was in turmoil and unable to help; there was the threat of new taxes; municipalities had been stripped of their authority; and tensions with the Americans were high. All of these issues were compounded by a governor in whom very few citizens had much confidence. Conditions were right for trouble. On August 3, 1837, a "Revolutionary Proclamation" was issued at Santa Cruz de la Cañada that declared its opposition to the department plan and made it clear that those who supported the plan were not welcome in New Mexico. The "Revolt of 1837" had begun.

On August 7, Governor Pérez and a small force left Santa Fe and marched to Santa Cruz to deal with what he described as "disorders and threatened seditions." The following morning, after encamping that night at the Pueblo of Pojoaque, Pérez and his men advanced a short distance to La Mesilla, just south of present-day Española and not far from the Pueblo of Santa Clara. There they encountered a large force of rebels and after a short but fierce battle, his small force was overwhelmed. Seeing his situation as hopeless, Pérez and a few of his men retreated to Santa Fe, but they did not find any support or refuge at the capital and decided to flee south to Mexico. That terrible night of August 8 to 9,1837, the besieged governor, along with the Abreus—Santiago, Ramón, and Marcelino—Secretary of Government Jesús María Alarid, the alférez Diego Saenz, Miguel Sena, José Loreto Escobar, and another man identified only as Ortega, were overtaken at various points along the road south of Santa Fe and killed. The chronicles tell us that Governor Pérez was decapitated by the rebels and his head paraded on a pole.

On June 14, 1901, the DAR dedicated a memorial to Governor Pérez and placed it along the road at Agua Fria near the site where he was killed. In 1970 the memorial was moved to the courtyard of the Palace of the Governors, but the DAR did not officially donate the memorial to the Museum of New Mexico until June 14, 2007. On that day, in a ceremony that closely replicated the 1901 dedication, palace and DAR officials, Pérez family descendants, La Sociedad Folklorica, military reenactors, and bagpipe players came together to rededicate this small token in the memory of Governor Albino Pérez. It seemed fitting that the memorial has its permanent home at the place where he assumed his office, delivered his inaugural address, and formulated the plans that led to his death. It was a fitting tribute not only to the man, but to a difficult and poorly understood period of our history.

CHAPTER TWO

Municipal Governments in Mexican-Era New Mexico

Municipal Governments

During the period that New Mexico was part of the Mexican Republic, there were many attempts to establish and maintain effective local governments throughout the territory. As a territory of Mexico, local authority in New Mexico was centralized in the territorial, or principal, government in Santa Fe under the leadership of a gefe politico, the region's civil leader whom we generally call a governor. This individual was appointed by the presiding executive in Mexico and served as president of an elected legislative and advisory body that met periodically in Santa Fe. This body functioned under various titles, such as the Diputación (1822), *Junta Departamental* (1835), and *Asamblea Departamental* (1842).

At the local level, late Spanish and Mexican law authorized ayuntamientos, which functioned as municipal governing bodies in the alcaldías, or districts. The number of these governing assemblies varied throughout the Mexican period, but generally the villas or principal cities of Santa Fe, Santa Cruz de la Cañada, and Alburquerque had a permanent ayuntamiento. Communities such as Abiquiú, Taos, Sandia, Tomé, Laguna, San Miguel del

Vado, and several others, also had functioning ayuntamientos at various times. These local governments are often described as a type of "city council," but in reality, they functioned more like county governments, with jurisdictions encompassing a district that included several communities. In 1841, for example, the jurisdiction of the ayuntamiento of Santa Fe included the city's neighborhoods of Torreón, Nuestra Señora de Guadalupe, and San Francisco, as well as the surrounding communities of La Cienega, Cieneguilla, Agua Fria, the Pueblo of Tesuque, Rio de Tesuque, and Galisteo. Even today those same communities fall within the modern political jurisdiction of the County of Santa Fe.

It is fascinating to read the documents of the period and see how local governments struggled with the same issues they still deal with in the twenty-first century. The records of proceedings, or minutes, of an ayuntamiento meeting in the 1830s or 1840s might have included a discussion on the duties of the *jues de policía*, the local law enforcement officer; complaints from citizens that local officials were not keeping the city streets and plaza clean; or the teacher vacancy in a local school. Their agendas were similar to those of any contemporary city council or county commission meeting.

Then, as now, a major point of discussion in local governments was money. New Mexico's governments were never able to establish a successful method of imposing and collecting direct taxes from its citizens and the diputación and ayuntamientos constantly sought sources of revenue to pay for the myriad responsibilities they had, such as paying expenses of the military, establishing schools, and paying teachers and salaries of government employees who frequently went unpaid due to a lack of revenue.

Consequently, most municipal regulations developed by the various ayuntamientos concentrated on raising revenue through licensing of business and imposing fines for a myriad of infractions—so much so that these municipal regulations were often called "revenue plans." An example of this are the ordinances developed for the municipality of Sandia by *jues de paz* (justice of the peace) Antonio Montoya and approved by the ayuntamiento of the villa of Albuquerque on February 20, 1840. The following are examples of the revenue items included:

> Persons not native to New Mexico were to pay two reales a day for the right to open a commercial store or winery;
>
> Persons who conducted, participated in, or simply were present at unlicensed games of chance were fined six, three, and one peso respectively;
>
> Persons whose livestock damaged agricultural fields were to pay damages and two reales fine for each incident;
>
> A license to conduct a dance was set at two reales. The fine for conducting a dance without said approval was four reales and twenty-four hours of arrest for the person responsible;
>
> A fine of three reales was to be paid by anyone who purposefully avoided his duty to work on the acequias or other assigned public service;
>
> Anyone who tapped into the *acequia madre* (mother/principal irrigation ditch) without authorization

> was fined one peso plus any additional punishment imposed by the mayordomo (overseer or ditch boss);
>
> Persons caught stealing from the fields of another were fined one peso, as well as being required to pay for damages and suffer twenty-four hours of arrest.

These local revenue plans were not overly ambitious or, for that matter, very regulatory. They emphasized small fines and license fees designed to exercise some social control while raising a modest amount of revenue for local needs. Few records exist to show how much revenue these statutes generated.

Municipal Elections at Santa Cruz de la Cañada, 1823–1824

Reviewing my research notes on Mexican-era government, my attention was drawn to a series of documents that provided details on how the ayuntamiento of Santa Cruz de la Cañada operated in the 1820s and early 1830s. The documents in question were several items found in the microfilm of the Sender Collection, a series of important documents that had been obtained by Kenneth Sender and offered for sale to the state in 1961. After the state's unsuccessful attempt to acquire the documents through replevin, they were subsequently acquired from another party in 1984.

The document that caught my attention was a March 4, 1823, report that Governor José Antonio Vizcarra was presiding over a meeting of the ayuntamiento in Santa Cruz to investigate accusations made against Santiago Abreu for alleged abuses during recent elections. Vizcarra apparently found no basis for the charges, publicly denounced the accuser, José del Carmen Fresques, as a "seditious disturber of the peace" and fined Fresques and three accomplices four reales each.

Subsequent documents provide details on how these municipal elections were conducted. On October 30, 1823, gefe politico Bartolomé Baca was in Santa Cruz presiding over the election of a new ayuntamiento. The first order of business appointed a secretary, Luis Cantu Lentes, and two scribes, Pedro Rafael Trujillo and Pedro Vigil. Then seventeen electors were selected from the general population in attendance, who would meet later to actually select the officers. The following is a list of these electors:

> Juaquín Valdes, Antonio García, Manuel Bustos, Andres Casillas, José Miguel Cordova, José María Tafolla, José Cristobal, García Julian Vigil, Felipe Archuleta, Mariano Dominguez, Luis Cantu Leiba, Felipe Romero, Rev. Manuel Rada, Pedro Rafael Trujillo, Gerbacio Ortega, Miguel Martín, Pedro Vigil

The following day, the seventeen electors met in a closed room to prepare a list of *hombres buenos* (good men) from which they would make their selections to the ayuntamiento. These electors then cast their ballots in secret and after tabulating the votes, Governor Baca announced the results to the public and asked if anyone had objections to the election of any of the officers. When no one objected, Baca proceeded to formalize the results:

First alcalde (*alcalde primero*)—Matías Ortiz; second alcalde, Gerbacio Ortega; regidores (council members) elected—Tomás Archuleta, Juan de Jesús Cruz, Francisco Montoya, Blas Quintana, and Felipe Romero. Considering that Gerbacio Ortega and Felipe Romero were the only two electors selected to the ayuntamiento suggests that the electors did not select exclusively from among themselves for higher offices and instead sought their leadership from a wider range of citizens whom they considered hombres buenos.

Finally, the oath of office was administered to the incoming officers, apparently by the outgoing alcalde primero. In 1826 Severiano Montoya placed a newly elected ayuntamiento in possession of their offices in the following form: "¿Jurias a Dios guardar y hacer guardar la Constitución Politica de los Estados Unidos Mejicanos, decretada y sancionada por el Congreso General constituyente en el año de 1824?" (Do you swear to God to guard and support the Political Constitution of the United Mexican States decreed and sanctioned by the General Congress constituted in the year of 1824?). After each responded "Sí juro" (I do swear), the proceedings were adjourned and the newly elected ayuntamiento of Santa Cruz de la Cañada proceeded as a group to the church for a Thanksgiving mass and a Te Deum by the parish priest.

Other documents indicate that things did not always go smoothly. One of the actions necessary in the transition of administrations was the requirement that the outgoing alcalde personally conduct or authorize an inventory of the council's archives and formally turn these over to the new administration.

While this was usually done without problems, in 1830 the new ayuntamiento convened but took no action because the archives remained in the custody of the ex-alcalde, José Ortega. The council called on the former secretary to arrange a formal inventory, but he refused to act because he had not been assured that Ortega would pay him to do so. Ortega concluded that he would do the inventory himself rather than pay the unnamed ex-secretary. Once that was settled, Ortega agreed to do the formal *entrega* (delivery or turning over) of the archives the following day.

Of special interest may be an 1830 listing of the twenty-two manzanas (political districts that can be considered similar to present-day precincts) that constituted the Santa Cruz de la Cañada jurisdiction. These settlements were listed for electoral purposes, possibly to assign how many electors each settlement was to provide for subsequent elections. Most of these communities retain a distinct identity to this day:

> Plaza Mayor, Plaza de San Pedro, Plaza de La Mesilla
> Pueblo of San Yldefonso Paraje de Jacona Cullamungue
> Pueblo of Nambe La Puebla, Plaza de los Dolores
> Plaza de la Cuchilla, Plaza del Cerro, El Potrero
> El Quemado Las Trampas, El Llano
> Rio De Chama, La Cuchilla Plaza de San José
> Plaza de San Antonio, Plaza de San Juan, La Vega,
> Chamizal

CHAPTER TWO

The 1829 Census

There were numerous censuses taken during the Spanish and Mexican periods of New Mexico history. Some of these, such as the Spanish censuses of 1750 and 1790 and the 1845 Mexican census, are a vast source of information, providing names, ages, and occupations of New Mexico's inhabitants. Others provide little more than the number of people living in a parish or community. These censuses have proven valuable sources of information for the thousands of individuals who do family research. Even an incomplete or fragmentary census can provide valuable details about how our New Mexican ancestors lived.

One such example is the Mexican census of 1829, which provides fragmentary information on only three places. However, these three represent the three principal geographical regions of the territory: Sabinal in the rio abajo; the jurisdiction of Cochiti in the middle Rio Grande Valley; and Santo Tomás Apostol de Abiquiú in the rio arriba. This census was supposed to collect not only population information, but also "the type and number of . . . crops and industry" found throughout New Mexico. What happened to the remainder of the census is a mystery, but from these surviving elements we can develop at least a limited view of life in these three regions.

The report from San Antonio del Sabinal, prepared by José María Lobato, shows only the adult male population of 207, of whom 176 were married, 27 were single, and 4 were widowers. Their livestock consisted of 100 cattle and 309 sheep and goats. Their crops, however, included 1,000 fanegas of corn, 300 of wheat, 6 of beans, 250 of chile, and 50 pesos worth of onions. They also produced 12 fanegas of cotton and 700 *manojos* (bundles) of *punche*, a native tobacco.

The report from Cochiti by the *alcalde constitucional* José Miguel Baca includes a table of population that is more detailed than that of Sabinal and lists 1,476 adults. Baca's report, however, provides no details on agriculture. He summarizes crop production for all the listed settlements under his jurisdiction as an abundance of corn and wheat, largely attributed to the availability of water for irrigation, except for Bajada, whose harvest was limited due to their lack of available water. The adult population listed is as follows:

Pueblo of Cochiti: 182 men, 190 women
Pueblo of Santo Domingo: 211 men, 216 women
Peña Blanca: 124 men, 127 women
Cañada de Cochiti: 125 men, 123 women
Zile: 48 men, 47 women
Bajada: 41 men, 42 women

The report for Abiquiú shows it as the most populated of the three, with a total of 3,611 "souls (*almas*)," including children (see figure 6), and provides the most detail on how the inhabitants made their living. The report by Miguel Quintana emphasizes the relative isolation of this frontier settlement, noting that the capital at Santa Fe was sixteen leagues (a league is approximately 2.6 miles) distant, and the nearest settlements to the east were five to six leagues away. He also explained there were no settlements west of Abiquiú except for *rancherías* (encampments) of Utes and Navajos.

Quintana noted that the temperature tended to be very cold and the terrain broken and mountainous, but the agricultural fields that were laid out along the rivers of the region tended to be quite fertile. He also indicated that agriculture was limited by a short summer season and because the ground was covered with snow during the winter.

Although the residents of Abiquiú planted wheat, corn, legumes, chile, and onions, Quintana felt most made their living with sheep and wool. While the planting and harvesting of crops took some time and labor every spring and fall, much of the summer and fall were devoted to the processing of wool and weaving a variety of cloth. Every winter these products and raw wool were taken to Chihuahua and Sonora to trade for mercantile goods. Others left Abiquiú every winter to hunt bison while some took the opportunity to trade with the various Native American nations along the frontier.

At first glance, this fragmentary census may seem to tell us very little beyond the rough statistics in its population tables. Upon closer review, however, these 1829 reports show that New Mexicans were a hardy and industrious frontier people who utilized the resources available to them to make their living.

Santa Fe's 1832 Municipal Regulations

The old adage which says that the more things change the more they stay the same applies to many things, but most especially to the way governments function. While New Mexico was under Mexican administration, the larger communities in the

	Solteros		Casados		Viudos		Totales	
	Hombres	Mugeres	Hombres	Mugeres	Hombres	Mugeres	Hombres	Mugeres
De 1 a 9 años	519.	518	...	- -	- -	-	519	518
De 10 á 25	236	234	179	278	8	23	413	535
De 25 a 40	199	196	343	244	10	19	553	459
De 40 a 50	75	48	64	61	18	21	157	130
De 50 Arriba	53	47	86	83	14	32	153	162
Totales	1082	1043	666	666	50.	95	1807	1804
Total general de Almas 3611								

Figure 6. Excerpt of table of census. Santo Tomás Apostol de Abiquíu, November 28, 1829. MANM: 1829, Miscellaneous, Census.

territory were governed by a local ayuntamiento, the equivalent of a contemporary town council, which was responsible for city government. As we can see by the following example of regulations passed by the ayuntamiento of Santa Fe in 1832, citizens and government officials of that era were concerned with many of the same issues that have taken up the agendas of city councils through the ages.

Several of the regulations, for example, concern themselves with public sanitation and obstruction of public roads, while others deal with the problems caused by stray dogs. It is also interesting to note that in 1832, local government also struggled with how to deal with the unemployed and those with no visible means of support, as well as protection for consumers and the moral well-being of children.

During the February 1832 session of the municipal council, a committee was appointed to draw up regulations for policing the city. On February 12, this *comisión de policía* submitted the following recommendations, which were approved by the ayuntamiento:

1. That the respective alcaldes of each neighborhood, accompanied by the regidores were to appoint men to sweep clean the plaza at least once every week.
2. Individuals who, contrary to the principals of good sanitation, parked their wagons and carts or placed poles and lumber on the plaza and streets were to be ordered to remove these to their own homes or other places where they did not obstruct free passage for those wishing to travel on the streets. Violators were to be punished to the severest extent allowed by law.
3. The sindico and police commission were to examine and review the weights, liquid measures, and the varas used by merchants, and to regulate commerce accordingly.
4. Alcaldes were to be scrupulous in severely punishing drunks who had nothing better to do than insult law-abiding citizens who were going about their business.
5. The carrying of short, presumably concealed, weapons such as knives and daggers, was prohibited and

punished according to the law. Apparently this type of weapon had been used in recent attacks on foreigners as well as other residents of the city.

6 & 7. A way was to be found to hire one or two persons to kill the stray dogs that threatened the citizens of Santa Fe and which presented the danger of rabies. If the city was unable to hire someone to kill stray dogs (as in unable to raise the funds to pay their salaries), dog owners were to be required to kill their dogs if they did not tie them up or take other actions to prevent them from getting loose.

8. The tribunal for vagabonds was to regularly gather all such individuals and put them to work, each according to their capabilities, in the homes of those who had work for them. Women without occupations were not to be exempted from this, as some were regularly seen in the streets at all hours of the night.

9. The officials who oversaw dances were to inspect the refreshment tables at these events to ensure the measurements used to serve them were not shortchanged and that the liquor sold was not diluted with a mix of any kind. Any seller who shortchanged his refreshments or diluted the liquor was to be ejected and held legally responsible for his actions.

10. Since diversions at fandangos (public dances) were felt to be part of society, these could not be prohibited if care was taken to assure Christian moderation in the music and that the music or entertainment did not include ballads or verses detrimental to children. Care

> was also to be taken that those who sponsored a *vaile panadero* (charity dance) did not shamelessly pocket the proceeds as had recently been the case.
> (signed) Juan García, 1st Constitutional Alcalde of Santa Fe.

The decree was to be made public by placing it on the door of the principal government building so it would come to the attention of all and none could claim ignorance when violators were punished with the full rigor of the law.

Celebrations at Tomé and Abiquiú, 1835

In early April 1834, Antonio López de Santa Anna decided to unretire from one of his frequent absences from the presidency of Mexico and returned to Mexico City to deal with the unrest that was developing over the liberal leanings of Vice President Vicente Gómez-Frias, whom he had left in charge of the presidency. In early 1835 the Mexican Congress ordered a reduction in the size of the militia forces in states, a move the government of Zacatecas resisted. Santa Anna, assuming command of the army, marched on the city and suppressed the resistance after a fierce battle.

Immediately following the victory, Santa Anna sent a series of circulars to the various governors informing them of the "disturbances to order that have been promoted by the authorities of Zacatecas" and the actions he took to suppress them. When news of these events reached Santa Fe, Governor Albino Pérez organized a celebration to commemorate the occasion. The June 17, 1835, celebration held at the capital featured military salvos, ringing of bells, a mass of thanks, *luminarias* (bonfires) in the streets, and general public rejoicing. Pérez also issued an order that all the ayuntamientos in New Mexico should commemorate the event with some form of public celebration.

Two reports of the resulting local celebrations have survived—one from Abiquiú and the other from Tomé. Both are wonderful documents that tell us a bit about how local governments functioned during the Mexican period in New Mexico. These reports were originally published in two separate "Voices From the Past" columns but are combined here to show how these two municipal governments—one in northern New Mexico and the other in the rio abajo—chose to observe the occasion. The following are my translations of the original documents to which some punctuation and accents not found in the original are added to make the translation more readable. We open with the July 9, 1835, report from Tomé.

The Tomé ayuntamiento, which consisted of José de Olona as president, the regidores (councilmen) José Manuel Sánchez, Enrique Chávez, José Gregorio Gallegos, and Juan Andrés Varela, sindico José Ignacio Salazar, and secretary José María Baca reported they had met that day, read the circulars received from Governor Pérez, and felt that the news of Santa Anna's victory over the insurgents had "filled all its members with great satisfaction." To commemorate the occasion, they appointed a committee to plan an appropriate celebration. That same day, the council approved the committee's recommendations and published the following report:

The committee charged with seeking the means to distribute the acts of solemnization of the triumph achieved over the dissidents by our government, as much to recognize the excitement as the great satisfaction that moves us, has found it convenient to issue the exposition in the following manner:

Without extending our reflections . . . on the happenings of our nation in general, for history is full of very recent dishonors . . . we were governed like a class of brutes, with rules dictated by capriciousness and persuasion carried out by force . . . until the year of 1821, when Independence was achieved and there appeared the splendor of Liberty; but this too was suffocated at the horizon by exaltation of the most harmful passions . . . which paralyzed for 13 years the magisterial march of beneficial influences. . . .

Does it not fill us with satisfaction and confidence of a leader who has declared himself in favor of social order, destroying the darkness that dims the desired benefits of instituting the bases or agreements that constrain men in society? Yes, dignified companions. . . . We congratulate ourselves, giving ourselves the benefit of being worthy, for after having suffered the most voracious torments, we see the port, [and] propose the following:

1. That a solemn mass be sung in thanks to the Supreme Being and also as a prayer for the complete triumph of the National prosperity, to be held on the 12th of this month, which day has been dedicated to the veneration of our Mexican Patroness [Our Lady of Guadalupe].
2. That there be vespers on the 11th with ringing of bells, "salvas," and illuminations to announce the solemnization.

3. During the mass, 15 salvos of firearms are to be fired, for which we have already arranged with the Señor cura and the Salazares of this vicinity.
4. Upon exiting Mass, the youth are to form a [illegible] and by means of songs and praise, express and acknowledge gratitude of the occasion.
5. That all classes of public diversions are permitted and in the afternoon a musical serenade is to be presented in the woods of this capital.
6. That there be illuminations during the hour of evening orations as the day before, and afterward, there be a public dance.

This is, overcoming all difficulties, what is to be done in compliance with such plausible news, so that you may do with that which you see most fit.

Tomé, July 9, 1835, Gallegos—Varela—Salazar

There is no documentation that tells us for certain what, if any, portion of the planned celebration was held. However, there is no doubt that the people of Tomé did in fact come together to take advantage of the opportunity to worship, give thanks, and celebrate for a few hours.

The following is the transcript of the July 21 report from the ayuntamiento of Santo Tomás Apostol of Abiquiú:

At this pueblo of Santo Tomás Apostol de Abiquiú, on the 21st day of the month of July of 1835, the citizen Francisco Estevan Vigil, *regidor de cano* (councilman of the day), acting as alcalde due to illness of the citizen Santiago Martines, the actual alcalde, to comply fully with the order and proclamation of the Honorable political and military chief, Colonel Don Albino Pérez, which he directed to this ayuntamiento, I called together all the members of this body to deal with the order that we most solemnly invoke the invitation of our president, Don Antonio López de Santa Ana, to celebrate the success and political actions he achieved in the city of Zacatecas, punishing the dissidents of that place and leaving its inhabitants in the peace and quiet of the laws dictated by the legislative bodies regarding the reform of the civil militia;

And said body being gathered in full and in full understanding of the matter, unanimous in their opinion, decided that to meet with the full compliance of this invitation to eulogize and cheer the invincible general, president Don Antonio López de Santa Ana, did invite the principal men of this jurisdiction, in writing, to voluntarily contribute in their persons and other means, so that this act may be carried out with due solemnity; which was acknowledged by the citizen Don Pedro Ignacio Gallegos with a dozen *coetes* (firecrackers or fireworks), and by the European Spaniard Don Damaso Lopes, with 46 charges of gunpowder. Orders were also issued to all the deputy policemen (*asistentes de policía*) to identify all those citizens in their plazas that have firearms, to present themselves with these today at three in the afternoon, the hour designated to carry out this act; and that all remaining citizens attend in their persons and that all these bring a load of pitch wood.

Which was complied with in full obedience except for the plazas of Rito Colorado due to the long distance [from

Abiquiú]; this body decided this act would be carried out and solemnized [later] at Rito Colorado because it is the most populous and seat of those places, to which all agreed.

The act was carried out at the designated hour with hanging decorations, ringing of bells, luminarias, fireworks, music, [and] poetry. Twenty men with firearms halted at the four corners of this pueblo, repeating "vivas" to our invincible general, President Don Antonio López de Santa Ana, and solemnizing these with discharges, musical interludes, and other such joyous actions and decorations provided by these citizens in recognition and full compliance with the orders of their superiors; principal among these being the elocution in honor of our invincible general, President Don Antonio López de Santa Ana, by the European Don Damaso Lopes; [said elocution] was toasted with *aguardiente* and the scattering of some coins, as well as those from this body [the ayuntamiento] with leftover powder and toasts of aguardiente until the evening oration that night, when all retired merrily to their homes.

Having the honor to communicate to your Excellency for this ayuntamiento, Abiquiú, July 21, 1835.

(signed)

Francisco Estevan Vigil, Regidor de cano

Manuel Lujan, Regidor 2°

Tomas Chacon, Regidor 3°

Jose Francisco Baldes, Regidor 4°

Pedro Leon Lujan, Regidor 5°

Antonio García, Regidor 6°

Marcos Delgado, Sindico

Hipolito Serrano, Secretario

Ayuntamiento Elections at Cochiti, 1836

There are hundreds of documents in our Spanish- and Mexican-era archives regarding the form and function of the ayuntamientos, the municipal councils that dealt with local issues. The number of communities that had these municipal councils varied, but as of 1828 Governor Manuel Armijo reported these to include the villas of Santa Fe, Albuquerque, and Santa Cruz de la Cañada, which served as *cabezas de partido*, much like capitals or county seats. The remaining ayuntamientos at that point were San Miguel del Bado, Cochiti, Xemes, Sandia, Ysleta, Tomé, Sabinal, Socorro, San Juan de los Caballeros, Taos, and Abiquiú.

There are hundreds of documents related to the activities of the ayuntamientos of Santa Fe and Santa Cruz de la Cañada. Most of the others listed above have some extant records, although to a lesser degree, and there is a scattering of records for a few others. Many of the records that have survived consist of reports of municipal elections and other correspondence that managed to make their way into our Spanish- and Mexican-era archives. Of special interest to genealogists are the names of hundreds of individuals that show up in these reports as nominees for local office and their eventual selection as regidores and ultimately, *alcaldes mayores*. Of even greater interest are the many records regarding contested elections.

Typical among these election records is the well-developed report submitted by Juan María Martín to Governor Albino Pérez describing the December 18, 1836, elections held for the ayuntamiento of the Pueblo of San Buenaventura de Cochiti. The report provides details of the "secondary election" conducted by electors that had been selected at a "primary election" by all the eligible voters in the community. These electors then convened to elect the members of the municipal council.

The report was submitted with an elegantly signed letter of transmittal by Martín as "President of the secondary electoral meeting of Cochiti," which notes that those elected would begin their terms of office within the New Year of 1837 and continues:

> In this Pueblo of San Buenaventura de Cochiti, at the 18th day of the month of December of 1836, the electors that constitute the secondary electoral meeting, reunited in the *casa consistorial* [town hall or court house] of the said pueblo for the renovation of the ayuntamiento for the upcoming year of 1837, proceeded with the naming of the President of the said meeting and two Secretaries . . . selected by absolute majority of votes, the [citizens] Juan Maria Martín, Francisco Alvino Aragon, and Juan de Dios Aragon [the names as written do not carry accent marks] . . . and the gentlemen selected taking their seats, we began with the election of Alcalde [as required by law].
>
> And the resolution made, resulted as elected the [citizen] C. Jose de Jesus Sanches, with 10 votes, and the two senior regidores remaining from the [previous] Ayuntamiento, immediately continued with the voting for 3rd Regidor and the vote being taken resulted in the election of Miguel Cabesa de Baca, with 10 votes; continuing with the fourth Regidor, the voting proceeded with the naming of Jose Archibeque, for having received 12 votes. Immediately proceeding with the voting for *Cindico Procurador* [Public Prosecutor] resulted in the naming

> of Juan Padia, with 13 votes, all in compliance with Art. 63 of the expressed law.
>
> And having presented all that is required . . . the meeting was dissolved at 2 in the afternoon, there being no objections after having made public [the results of said election].
>
> [Signed] Juan Ma. Martin, President, Francisco Alvino Aragon, 1st Secty., Juan de Dios Aguilar, 2nd Secty."

Other extant records related to the Cochiti ayuntamiento reveal a troubling issue. Ayuntamientos were required to maintain archives of their proceedings, but only a limited number of these still exist. The surviving records for the Cochiti ayuntamiento include an inventory dated July 10, 1827, that lists more than two hundred documents that existed in their municipal archives covering the period 1820 through 1827. The inventory includes books of decrees, a copy of the Mexican Federal Constitution, folios of governor's decrees and correspondence, and references to civil suits involving the Pueblo of Cochiti. Several entries list wheat and corn collected by the ayuntamiento as revenue and payments made to the municipal council's secretary and purchase of paper utilizing these crops.

These municipal officers seemed diligent in maintaining an official archive and remitting required reports and information to Santa Fe. So what became of the documents listed in the archives inventory? Is it possible portions still survive in some former official's home? Or tragically, as happened to so many of New Mexico's own official archives, were they thrown out when someone decided they had no value? Like with so much of our history, all we can say is, ¿Quién sabe?

An Uprising at Cebolleta, 1839

While paging through the bound volumes of *Archivo de la Nación* (AGN) copies of documents at the University of New Mexico, I came across a series of documents filed under the tantalizing title, "Sobre una conspiracion descubrida en N. Mexico—1839" (Regarding a conspiracy discovered in New Mexico, 1839). This certainly seemed to have the makings of a story.

The documents consist of letters describing an uprising at the western frontier settlement of Cebolleta and the efforts of local officials to suppress it. The AGN series ends with a letter by Governor Manuel Armijo regarding the arrest and imprisonment of the conspirators, but despite the obviously serious nature of the situation, I have found only one document in our Mexican Archives of New Mexico that mentions this "conspiracy."

The AGN documents open with a July 1, 1839, report from school teacher and local justice of the peace (*juez de barrio*) Vicente Margarito Hernández, noting that several individuals had gone to his home to protest unspecified "injuries" they had incurred due to "bad administration of justice" by local officials. They also threatened to release, by force of arms, Joaqúin Candelaria, who was being held in jail for unspecified reasons. In a later report, Hernández identified the individuals who went to his house as Juan Agustín Peralta, Pedro Chaves,

Marcos Jaramillo, Francisco Chaves, José Chaves, José Rafael García, and Juan Martín.

Upon receiving notice of the issue, Second District (rio abajo) Prefect Antonio Sandoval wrote to Governor Armijo and suggested the "conspirators" may have been instigating the Pueblo Indians of Laguna and Acoma to join the protest or uprising.

Meanwhile, José Francisco Chaves Baca, writing from the *jusgado* (court or courtroom) of Cebolleta, identified Juan Agustín Peralta as one of the principal "revolutionaries" and ordered the sergeant of militia, Juan García, to summon fifty men and attempt to convince Peralta to turn himself in and answer to charges that he had refused to report for militia duty and participate in a recent Navajo campaign with the excuse that he was sick. Sergeant García, the cabos Rafael Sanches, Pablo Sandoval, José Francisco Aragón, and soldier Francisco Aragón proceeded to Cebolleta with orders to arrest Peralta if he further resisted. When they arrived at Cebolleta and attempted to effect an arrest, they found that Peralta's neighbors, possibly those who had initially protested at Hernandez's house, had gathered in his support and insisted that they too were tired of enduring the authority of an unidentified judicial official (possibly Chaves Baca) and would submit only under force of arms.

The following day, July 5, Governor Armijo, obviously concerned with the escalating local resistance to authority, ordered the Inspector de Milicias Rurales (Inspector of Rural Militia), Captain Gregorio Ortiz, to put together a force of two hundred men and proceed at once to Cebolleta to determine what forces the rebels had and, if it was too large to overcome, inform Armijo by special messenger. If Ortiz managed to capture the revolutionaries, he was to escort them all to Santa Fe, making sure Cebolleta remained "in good order and obedient to the law." In a subsequent July 7 report to Prefect Sandoval that is worthy of a separate article, José Francisco Chaves Baca detailed his efforts to quell the uprising without resorting to violence, noting he met with local citizens he considered (without naming them) "men . . . of good name," as well as the leadership of the pueblos of Laguna and Acoma and convinced them that support for the unfaithful citizens of Cebolleta was unmerited.

Chaves Baca's persuasive diplomacy apparently convinced the principal leaders of the uprising to surrender, and two days later, Prefect Antonio Sandoval reported he and an escort of militia from Los Padillas were on their way to Santa Fe with the three principal leaders, Juan Agustín Peralta, Ramón Sanches, and Pedro Chaves.

Extant records tell us very little about what became of these men. The final document of the AGN material is a letter dated July 28, 1839, from Governor Armijo addressed to the Minister of Interior in Mexico. The letter notes that Armijo was enclosing copies of the relevant documents concerning the uprising and adds only that the prisoners were "expunging their crime" in jail at Santa Fe and were going to stay there until they admitted their crime and repented. A marginal notation dated later that year suggests that Mexico's president had approved the actions taken to suppress the rebellion and imprison the leadership.

The only Mexican Archives of New Mexico document related to this Cebolleta uprising is a July 31, 1839, report from Governor Armijo to the *comandante general* in Chihuahua confirming that the leaders were being held securely in Santa Fe and that order had been restored to the region. The historical record is silent on what happened to the three prisoners. There is no record of judicial proceedings or subsequent sentencing. It is possible Peralta, Sanches, and Chaves simply relented to Governor Armijo's demand that they admit their guilt and repent and were released to continue with their lives at Cebolleta, their brief defiance to authority largely forgotten.

Report from Santa Clara, 1840

On March 14, 1840, Juan Cristobal García, the interim justice of the peace for the jurisdiction of the Pueblo of Santa Clara submitted a fascinating report to Governor Manuel Armijo. The document is less than four pages long but is one of the most complete descriptions of the mineral, agricultural, and water resources of the rio arriba for this period. The document was apparently prepared in response to a general call for such information from throughout New Mexico.

Beginning with Santa Clara and working his way north, García identified the settlements in his *partido*, or jurisdiction, as Mi Señora de Guadalupe, two San Pedros, San Juan, Santa Rosalia, San Antonio, San Jose, San Francisco, La Pura y Limpia Consepcion, and finally, to the west, the settlement of La Divina Pastura. Santa Clara and San Pedro are the only remaining recognizable community names that have survived.

García opens his report by noting that it was prepared from his own limited knowledge of the subjects as well as from

Figure 7. "The Tewa Pueblo of K'Hapóo or Santa Clara." *Fourteenth Annual Report of the Bureau of Ethnology, 1892–1893* (Government Printing Office, 1896), 587.

information obtained from several inhabitants more familiar than he with the resources of the district. In the short opening section on mineral resources, García noted that his informants had no knowledge of silver, gold, copper, lead, steel, coal, or other precious metals or minerals in the region. The following section of agriculture, however, details the various crops grown in the valley, when they were planted and harvested, and their worth.

Wheat, for example, was planted in March, harvested in August, and valued at 2 pesos per fanega; barley was planted in March, harvested in July, and valued at between 12 reales (a peso and a half) and 2 pesos per fanega; corn was planted in April, harvested in October, and valued at 2 pesos per fanega;

pinto and garbanzo beans were planted in March, harvested in September, and valued at 3–4 pesos per fanega. Wheat and corn were the most abundant and important of these crops.

Other crops included chile, horse beans (*abas*), peas, lentils, garlic, and punche, the native tobacco. Onions were valued at 100 per peso, and garlic at 120 per peso. Melons and watermelons sold at 8 for 2 reales. Orchards produced apricots, peaches, apples, and plums. The apricots and peaches were valued at 12 reales per fanega, but the value of the apples and plums was not given.

The report also described a division of labor between men and women. Men did the planting, dug ditches, irrigated the fields, and harvested the crops. Following the harvest, men worked with wool, presumably in weaving, but García was not specific about this. Women devoted their time to grinding corn and wheat, while others wove, spun wool, and made stockings.

The principal sources of irrigation were the Rio del Norte (Rio Grande) and the Chama, both of which flowed rapidly and provided abundant water. The width of these rivers varied from five hundred varas, during the spring runoff, to little more than one hundred at its low point, at which the flow was less than two feet deep. These waters provided power for *molinos* (grist mills), but he did not mention their number or locations. García also noted that while these rivers might be considered navigable, navigation consisted of crossing from one shore to the other with canoes constructed from pine trees, and were five to six varas long and one and a half wide.

The hills and mountains flanking the valley provided abundant pasture, and the surrounding mesas and broken terrain were covered with piñon and cedar (juniper). The mountains

Figure 8. This *molino* from Taos was typical of the era's *acequia* (irrigation ditch) water-powered grist mills. "Exterior of flour mill, Taos, NM." Thayer Publishing Co. postcard, Robert J. Tórrez Collection.

west of Santa Clara were also the source of the Santa Clara River, which was fed by three crystal-clear springs. What was not utilized for irrigation by the Pueblo of Santa Clara flowed into the Rio del Norte. These mountains were also the source of water that flowed occasionally through the arroyo known as the Rio del Oso before flow disappeared into the sandy bottom of the arroyo.

The exact purpose of García's report is not clear but may have been part of the information gathered for a map of the rio arriba that Governor Manuel Armijo submitted to the federal government in Mexico in 1841. Tragically, the map Armijo referred to has been lost, as have the other reports on which the map was based. The map and these reports would have provided us with an extraordinary look at New Mexico's resources for this period of our history. For now, we must be thankful that at least Juan Cristóbal García's report survived to enhance our knowledge about a small part of the Rio Grande Valley in the vicinity of what is now Española.

Report from Santo Domingo, 1845

Among the numerous documents that provide information about and glimpses into New Mexico's history is a report submitted by Manuel Vizcarra from Peña Blanca dated April 16, 1845. The document has a long and weighty title that begins with "Noticia analistica de los datos nesesarios y conbenientes para la formacion de la Estadistica del Departamento" (Analytical Report of the data necessary for Developing Statistics of the Department). This report from the political jurisdiction of Santo Domingo is meant to be a part of a larger study ordered by the Department Assembly to gather information about New Mexico's natural resources and potential for economic development. Unfortunately, reports from other regions of the territory have apparently not survived, and the compiled report, presumably submitted to the central government, is not in New Mexico's archives. Vizcarra's report provides a snapshot of how one government official viewed a part of the middle Rio Grande Valley more than a century and a half ago.

Figure 9. Pueblo of Santo Domingo. J. W. Abert, *Abert's New Mexico Report, 1846–'47*, (Horn & Wallace, Publishers, 1962), 69.

Vizcarra indicated that the region under his jurisdiction consisted of a strip five leagues (about twelve miles) wide and approximately thirteen leagues (more than thirty miles) in length along the Rio del Norte (Rio Grande), stretching from the Rio de los Frijoles in the north to Angostura in the south. He described the landscape as "mostly broken" with mountain ranges known as El Valle and Mesa de San Felipe located to the north and west, respectively. Landmarks to the east and south included the peaks of Juana Lopes, Sierra del Oro, and Sierra Sandia. These mountain ranges were covered with abundant forests that provided wood, lumber, pasture, and some permanent waters.

The Rio del Norte (Rio Grande) was the only river that flowed through the jurisdiction. Most of the population was located among the banks of this waterway, which was lined by cottonwood trees and agricultural fields. There were no tributaries that fed or branches that came off the river. Its current was constant, with no waterfalls or cascades that filtered or reduced its flow, which was abundant in May and June, and it reverted to its natural state the rest of the year.

There were no thermometers available to provide data on temperature, but in common terms, Vizcarra felt the climate was similar to many parts of the territory. Fruit trees and other greenery began to flower in April and May, and the season ended in October at the same time as the migratory birds arrived. The first frosts occurred in November and continued through February. Snow covered the peaks and lowlands for several days at a time but occasionally lasted for months without melting. Most days were clear and windy, and the breezes carried no strange or disagreeable odors. Rains came in April and lasted through June. During the dry months, strong winds from the south and west often damaged fields, especially when these were accompanied by hail.

A few specimens of fine lead found in the Cañada de Peralta were the only minerals Vizcarra knew about, but he indicated that it was common knowledge these mountains contained copper mines that were not developed for lack of interest. Near Los Alamitos, some pieces of white stone that looked like the crystals used to cut glass had been found, which were thought to be bits of diamond.

Vegetation consisted of trees, vines, and timber essential for firewood, and for building homes and bridges. Fruits, flowers, leaves, fibers, grapes, and wild gum were abundant. Certain of these were utilized to make dyes and others for balsams and medicinal ointments for humans and livestock.

The settlements that recognized Santo Domingo as its head consisted of the pueblos of Santo Domingo, Cochiti, and San Felipe, along with the Spanish settlements of Peña Blanca, Cañada de Cochiti, Zile, Bajada de San Miguel, Cubero, Algodones, Angostura, and Tejón. The population totaled 3,135 inhabitants, whose main occupation was agriculture and the production of wool. All the land in this jurisdiction was dedicated to agricultural pursuits, but since much of the land was privately owned, most of it was utilized for pasture and the remainder produced enough for the families to subsist. The livestock consisted of 2,021 cattle, 551 horses and mules, 29,800 sheep, and 8,000 others, presumably goats. Many of these were held in partido, a system in which a sheep owner leased a flock of sheep to an individual in exchange for a percentage of lambs and wool every year.

Vizcarra did not know the name of the language the Pueblo Indians spoke and described it only as "very different from Castilian," the principal language spoken in the cities, ranches, and countryside. None of these pueblos and settlements had an ayuntamiento, or town council. The jurisdiction had no commercial societies, factories, medical facilities, or financial institutions such as banks. Education was provided by three small primary schools that had recently been established. The church and chapels in the pueblos and Peña Blanca were the only public buildings, and all were constructed of earth and ordinary timber.

Measuring the Santo Domingo Pueblo League, 1844

In a document dated May 19, 1841, Miguel Antonio Lobato entered into an agreement with the "governors, generals, and principal men" of the Tewa pueblos of San Juan, Santa Clara, San Yldefonso, Pojoaque, Nambe, Tesuque, and Sandia by which the pueblos granted Lobato substantial authority to conduct business on their behalf (see "A Power of Attorney, 1841," p. 200). At some point during this period, Lobato must have entered into a similar agreement with the Pueblo of Santo Domingo because in a document dated August 23, 1844, he presented himself as Santo Domingo's legal representative and submitted a petition to Governor Mariano Martínez asking for a measurement and confirmation of Santo Domingo's Pueblo League.

Lobato indicated that the *mojoneras* (monuments) that marked the boundaries of the pueblo had gone missing, causing several complaints about encroachment on pueblo lands by an adjoining property owner (*conlindante*), José de Jesús Sanches. To avoid a costly legal suit, Lobato asked the governor to order the pueblo league be measured "by the four winds," as had been done by the alcalde Juan José Gutierres in 1815. Lobato seems to suggest a new measurement was needed because documents issued that year to the pueblo by Governor Alberto Maynez had

Figure 10. Brass Mexican-era standard vara. "Mexican Vara." National Institute of Standards and Technology Digital Collections, Information Services Office, 2017. Beautiful Measures Exhibit. Gaithersburg, MD.

Figure 10a. Mexican eagle stamp on brass vara above.

been lost or misplaced and were not found in the archives kept by the government in Santa Fe.

On August 26, 1844, Governor Martínez ordered the prefect, Francisco Sarracino, to notify all the adjoining property owners of the impending pueblo league measurement, and three days later Sarracino notified conlindantes Vicente Baca and José de Jesús Sanches to be at Santo Domingo on September 3.

On that day Sarracino along with his secretary, Clemente Sarracino, and citizens José Alejandro Santistevan and Juan Arze, who were to serve as witnesses to the legitimacy of the proceedings, gathered at the cemetery of the Pueblo of Santo Domingo, where they were joined by conlindantes Vicente Baca and José Benito Sanches (who appeared on behalf of his father, José de Jesús Sanches). With Lobato present as representative of the pueblo, they measured out a rope or cord (often referred to as a *cordel*) of fifty varas (which he described as a *varilla*) and then "with great care" measured out one hundred varillas to the north, crossing the Rio del Norte once, totaling the five thousand varas that constituted the pueblo league.

At that point Sarracino ordered a monument of stone be placed on the spot where the 5,000 varas had been measured and two trenches dug in the form of a cross, which were to be filled with stones. Lobato also noted that based on information from village elders, they located remnants of previous monuments nearby, confirming the accuracy of the current measurement. Sarracino concluded his task by submitting his report to Governor Martínez, who ordered copies sent to all interested parties.

The Santo Domingo league had no doubt been measured before, as noted by Sarracino's comment that remnants of previous markers had been found in the immediate vicinity of the one done in 1844. One of the earliest descriptions regarding measurement of the pueblo league is found in a document in our Spanish archives dated June 8, 1722. That day, Alphonso Real de Aguilar reported that on orders from Governor Juan Domingo Bustamante, he measured the pueblo league between Santo Domingo and Cochiti.

Real de Aguilar's report stems from a dispute regarding property located between the two pueblos that doña Juana Baca had sold to Cochiti. Real de Aguilar decided to measure both pueblos' leagues and then split any intervening property evenly between the two, and according to his report, both pueblos agreed to the arrangement.

Real de Aguilar does not specify on what date he carried out the measurements, but he and his assistants, with witnesses from both pueblos present, utilized a cordel of unspecified length, starting from the center of the plaza of Santo Domingo, measured 5,000 varas north toward Cochiti, and placed a marker on the spot. Then, from Cochiti, they repeated the process south 5,000 varas toward Santo Domingo. That left 1,600 varas in the intervening space, which he divided into two 800-vara portions. Real de Aguilar does not mention if he issued any documents to the pueblos concerning this transaction.

It is notable that neither the 1722 nor the 1844 measurement mentioned the eastern or western boundaries of the pueblos. Only the north-south width was measured. I have not seen the original grant documents for either pueblo but it is likely that the east-west boundaries are stated not in varas but in natural features of the landscape. If so, that would be typical of the manner in which land grants were issued and their boundaries described, during these eras. What intrigues me personally is whether remnants of the various boundary monuments that have been erected over the past centuries still exist.

Political Jurisdictions in New Mexico, 1844–1846

When Stephen Watts Kearny enacted the new system of American law commonly known as the Kearny Code in 1846, he established the basis for New Mexico's original seven counties and the "circuit" or District Court system. The seven counties he designated were Santa Fe, San Miguel del Bado, Rio Arriba, Taos, Santa Ana, Bernalillo, and Valencia. According to the Kearny Code, these seven political subdivisions were based on the "counties and districts" as established by New Mexico's Department Assembly on June 17, 1844.

For most of its history, New Mexico was traditionally divided into two political, geographic, and some say social jurisdictions. The north was considered the rio arriba, or upper river district, and the south was the rio abajo, or lower river region. The dividing line between these two jurisdictions is generally considered to be in the vicinity of the bajada, the descent of the camino real into the Rio Grande Valley that we still call La Bajada (some suggest it is the bajada only as you travel south and should be the *subida*, or ascent, as you travel north). It should also be noted that during the Spanish era the northern jurisdiction was generally not referred to as rio arriba, but rather, simply as *el*

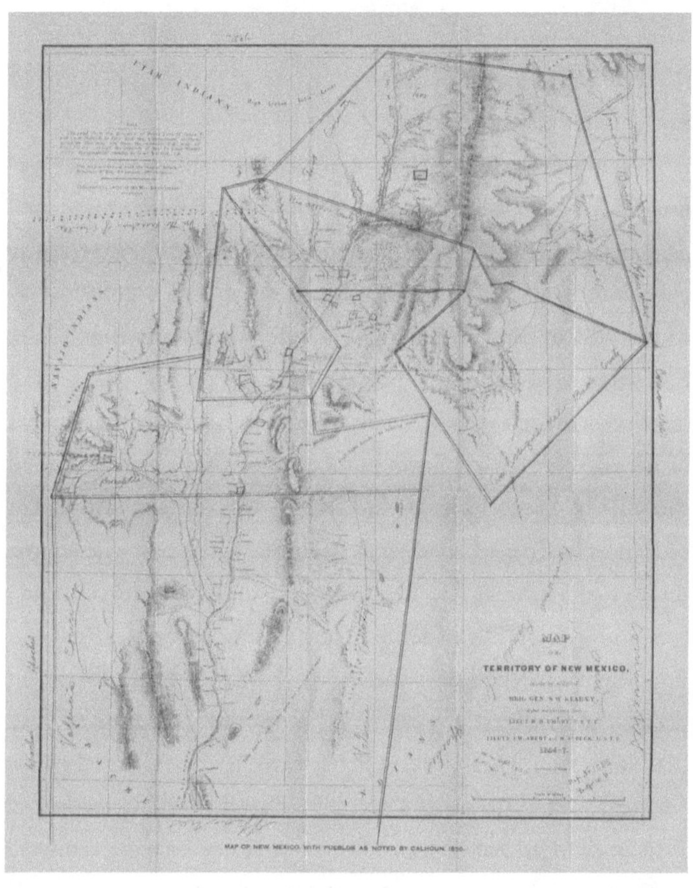

Figure 11. Map of the Territory of New Mexico made by order of Brig. General S. W. Kearny. Map No. 2 insert in Annie Heloise Able, editor, *The Official Correspondence of James S. Calhoun* (Government Printing Office, 1915).

norte, or the north. Until the mid-nineteenth century, the name rio arriba more properly referred to one of the villages north of present-day Española.

New Mexico's political jurisdictions became better defined during the early Mexican period. In 1823 the territorial diputación divided the province into four districts referred to as *partidas* or *partidos*. The first district consisted of the capital city of the villa of Santa Fe, which included the ayuntamientos of San Miguel del Bado, Cochiti, Jemez, and Alameda. The second district included the villa of Albuquerque and its ayuntamientos of Isleta, Tomé, Belen, Socorro, and Laguna. The third included the villa of Santa Cruz de la Cañada and the ayuntamientos of San Juan de los Caballeros, Abiquiú, and Taos. The fourth district of Paso del Rio Del Norte included the surrounding communities of Isleta (del Sur) and San Lorenzo del Real.

There were changes to these jurisdictions over the subsequent decade, not the least of which was the formal separation of Paso del Norte from New Mexico in the early 1830s. When the new Mexican constitution of 1836 introduced the "Departmental Plan," it changed New Mexico from a "territory" to a "department," and renamed the legislative assembly as the Junta Departamental (Department Assembly). The plan also reorganized New Mexico into two very large political jurisdictions, designated as the First District and the Second District. The First District, with the capital at Santa Fe designated as the *cabesera*, or head, consisted of all the alcaldías of what we would today consider the rio arriba of northern New Mexico, extending from Santa Fe north to Taos, and east to San Miguel del Bado. The Second District, with Albuquerque as its cabesera, consisted of the region we easily recognize as the rio abajo, beginning with Cochiti and extending south to Socorro, and west to the pueblos of Acoma and Zuni. Each district was headed by a prefect appointed by the governor.

These political jurisdictions remained basically unchanged until June 17, 1844, when the Department Assembly reorganized New Mexico into three districts designated as the northern, central, and southwest districts. These districts were further divided into seven partidas that correspond roughly to the political jurisdictions we today call counties. The central district consisted of the partidas of Santa Fe, Santa Ana, and San Miguel; the northern district included the partidas of Rio Arriba and Taos; and the southwest district consisted of the partidas of Valencia and Bernalillo. This is the Mexican legislation referred to in the Kearny Code.

Less than a month later, however, on July 5, 1844, the assembly modified their earlier legislation on political divisions. They designated the city of Santa Fe, plaza of Los Luceros, and plaza of Tomé as the heads of their respective districts. The decree further divided each district into smaller jurisdictions that can be compared to precincts, and assigned a *jues de paz*, or justice of the peace, to each.

Two days later, on July 7, the Assembly again amended the legislation. Citing "an error" in the July 5 statute, they repealed Los Luceros and Valencia as district seats and designated the villas of Santa Cruz de la Cañada and Albuquerque in their place as "*cabezera de Distrito y Partido*."

When the men who drafted what became the Kearny Code looked at the Mexican-period legislation to determine political jurisdictions under the new American government, they apparently missed or ignored the July 5 and July 7 amendments to the June 17, 1844, legislation cited in the Kearny Code. If they had taken the amendments into account, Santa Cruz de la Cañada would have been the county seat for Rio Arriba instead of Los Luceros, and Albuquerque the seat for Bernalillo County instead of Bernalillo.

CHAPTER THREE

A Constant State of War

Captain Francisco Salazar's 1821 Expedition

Two centuries ago in May of 1821, Captain Francisco Salazar undertook a three-week expedition to eastern New Mexico on the orders of Governor Facundo Melgares. The journal of his expedition is a simple four-page document found in the Spanish Archives of New Mexico but added here because the expedition unfolded just as Mexico was entering the final stages of achieving its independence from Spain and serves as an example of the resources New Mexico would continue to expend to defend itself from the incessant raids of the tribes that surrounded the territory.

Two weeks before Captain Salazar set out, a squad of militia clashed with some hostiles from *las Naciones del Norte,* one of the Northern Plains Tribes, somewhere along New Mexico's eastern frontier. The alférez Fernando Delgado and soldiers Tomás Saenz and Antonio Pacheco were killed in the encounter, and their bodies buried near the scene of the battle. Governor Melgares's orders and instructions to Captain Salazar are not in the archives, but it appears he was sent to track and find the unidentified hostiles. Salazar seems to have been the right man for the job. He was an experienced frontier soldier from Abiquiú. His *hoja de servicio,* or service record, shows that at the time of this 1821 expedition, he was sixty years old and had recently served in three campaigns between 1817 and 1819.

Salazar left Abiquiú early, the morning of May 2, 1821, and headed east toward Lo de Mora. He arrived at Picuris the following afternoon and in the early morning of May 4, made his way across the mountains to Lo de Mora, where he took command of one hundred sixty militia and presidio soldiers, which constituted his scouting expedition.

The expedition set out from Mora on May 6 and proceeded east for two days. His daily journal entries note that these first days passed *sin novedad,* with nothing of importance to report. The afternoon of May 8, two men from Santa Barbara (possibly from the Peñasco area) arrived with a message from Governor Melgares. Captain Salazar does not state what the message was, but at 4:00 a.m. on May 9, "in compliance with the order of my superior," he and his men headed northeast to a point between Ocaté and the "Cienega de los Santa Claras," possibly in the direction of present-day Wagon Mound. The following day, the expedition turned south toward the junction of the Sapello and Mora Rivers near today's Watrous, where they encountered a trail several days old that had been made by a considerable herd of horses and cattle moving north. They followed the trail about fifteen leagues (a league is approximately 2.6 miles) but found the trail badly deteriorated because of rainy weather and turned back, camping at a site slightly north or northwest of present-day Las Vegas, on the night of May 11.

At 1:00 a.m. on May 12, Captain Salazar sent out two scouting parties. A foot patrol of twenty-five men under the command of the cabo Antonio Armijo went south toward Tecolote, where Armijo encountered two badly weathered trails that proved useless to follow. Armijo and the second scout of thirty mounted men commanded by the cabo Juan Baca returned to camp at about 3:00 p.m. that same day with nothing significant to report, except for two stray bulls they encountered along the way. One of the bulls reportedly "*seles yso bravo*" (went wild on them) and they had to kill it. The other bull was reportedly returned to its owner. Indications are, the bull they killed provided some welcome fresh meat for the expedition.

After the scouts returned to camp, Captain Salazar set out to where the alférez Fernando Delgado and the two soldiers killed the previous month were buried. He discovered that animals had tried to dig up the remains, so he secured the graves with large mounds of dirt. On June 16, 1821, a month after Salazar secured the grave site, the remains (*los huesos*, according to the burial record) of Delgado, Saenz, and Pacheco were retrieved and reburied at the Castrense, the military chapel in Santa Fe. There is no indication who recovered the remains for reburial.

Early in the morning on May 13, the expedition made its way back to Mora, arriving there late that night. Along the way they encountered a number of trails, but by then the expedition was showing signs of fatigue. Groups of militia began to ask to be relieved of duty and allowed to return to their homes so they could get back to their spring planting. Over the next few days, Salazar sent out small groups of men to scout the area around Mora and Golondrinas, but these accomplished nothing. On May 19 a messenger arrived, apparently with orders for Salazar to send the men home. At daybreak, May 20, Salazar issued orders for the militia to go home and distributed several fanegas of wheat to each contingent according to the number of men each alcaldía had provided. Captain Salazar's last entry is dated May 21, 1821, in which he simply states that he left camp at one o'clock in the morning and arrived at Picuris at noon that same day. The expedition was over; nothing of significance had been accomplished, but everyone apparently went home safely.

Decline of the New Mexico Presidio

The presidio, the military garrison in Santa Fe, was one of the defining elements of the Spanish and Mexican presence in New Mexico. Permanently established following the 1692–1693 reconquista of Diego de Vargas, this *Companía Veterana de Caballería del Real Presidio de Santa Fe* (Veteran Company of Cavalry of the Royal Garrison of Santa Fe) served until September of 1821. As 1821 came to a close, the garrison consisted of ninety-nine officers and men, five interpreters, and thirty-six aggregated invalidos, or retired soldiers. Aside from a small reduction in numbers from the Spanish period, military records and musters show little change in structure, organization, or routine of the presidio during the months following Mexican independence. Musters show that the Spanish military garrison at Santa Fe seamlessly evolved into the *Companía Veterana de Caballería, Presidio Nacional de Santa Fe* (Veteran Company of Cavalry, National Garrison of Santa Fe).

This period also experienced the worsening of a problem that transcended governments—the persistent problem of how to pay the troops. Presidio payroll accounts show that salaries for the company were scrupulously budgeted every year. However, indications are, these salaries were seldom paid in full at any time during the late Spanish or Mexican period. The detailed salary accounts of individual soldiers and officers show an annual credit for each salary, along with debits for goods, clothing, sundry items, and cash given to the individuals. Most of these accounts show clearly that a soldier with any tenure at all built up significant credits for which they were never paid in full.

By late 1823, an inability to pay the troops is clearly reflected in the military, executive, and legislative records in New Mexico's Mexican-era archives. That year, Governor Bartolomé Baca received a desperate appeal from the presidio military commander for assistance to provide for his troops. Baca referred the petition to the diputación, but all they could do was suggest that Baca appeal for relief from the superior government in Mexico. In late 1824 the desperate financial status of the territory prompted the diputación to consider a proposal to abolish the garrison and retain only thirty men at selected outposts for basic defense.

Reductions in the forces became real in the early 1830s. The June 1835 muster shows forty-one soldiers on leave without pay. According to Captain José Caballero, these men were simply sent home due to the lack of funds to feed and supply them. By February 1837, Governor Albino Pérez reported that he had been forced to dismiss all the troops except for two cabos and seven soldiers, which were all he could support "on his own account." He conceded that this left the frontier completely undefended, but he could do nothing more about it at the time. None of these reports explain how the troops supported themselves during these "layoffs."

The situation did not improve substantially for years. On May 8, 1839, Governor Manuel Armijo received an inquiry from the Ministerio de Guerra in Mexico asking why troop musters had not been submitted. Governor Armijo responded that no reports had been submitted because there was not a single soldier under arms in New Mexico. He had "retired" or sent the entire company to their homes because there were no funds to pay them. A year later, improved revenue from the American commercial caravans and some funds from the government in Mexico enabled the presidio to maintain a total of sixty men and officers—forty-six at Santa Fe, ten at Taos, and four at San Miguel del Bado.

In addition to ongoing problems with inadequate revenues and the persistent destitution of its troops, the status of the presidio was further diminished by the fact that for most of the Mexican period, this proud cavalry unit, whose roots dated back to the seventeenth century, was reduced to infantry. An inventory of the presidio property dated November 22, 1822, shows that the garrison had 132 horses and 48 mules available for service. However, the horse herd was apparently never replenished from this point and horses and mules needed for campaigns often were provided through levies imposed on the citizens of the province, as the need arose. A review of the presidio troops stationed at Taos in October 1841, for example, shows that the only mount available for the entire garrison was one mule belonging to one of the sergeants.

Despite all these problems, the men of the presidio served honorably, when given the opportunity and resources to do so. For two and half centuries, they put their lives on the line in dozens of campaigns against Native American raiders and performing dangerous outpost duties. They remained loyal to the government in the difficult times of 1837, faced the Texans in 1841 and 1843, and were dutifully prepared to defend against the American invasion of August 1846. Their sense of duty and ability to overcome hardships is reflected in the service records of individuals who worked their way through the ranks and became some of the most prominent men in New Mexico history.

San Miguel del Bado—Defending the Eastern Frontier

New Mexico's frontiers were vast and forbidding places in the eighteenth century. The Taos region was settled permanently, although not extensively, by the early 1700s and Santa Rosa de Lima and Santo Tomás Apostol de Abiquiú were established along the northwest frontier by the 1750s. In eastern New Mexico, settlements spread along the Rio Pecos but did not venture far from the parent communities south of Pecos until early in the nineteenth century. Through much of this period San Miguel del Bado (historically, the name was usually spelled with a "B" although it is usually spelled "Vado" today) was the principal settlement along this easternmost frontier.

The basic difficulties of life on the frontier were made more so by the dangers settlers faced from the various Native American tribes that regularly raided their flocks, stole livestock, killed settlers, and kidnapped women and children. These problems eventually led to a decision by the Mexican government to

Figure 12. San Miguel del Bado. Abert, *Abert's New Mexico Report, 1846–'47*, 39.

establish a permanent *destacamento,* a military outpost at San Miguel to help protect the settlements there.

The practice of stationing presidio soldiers at San Miguel del Bado (whose name derives from the *bado,* or crossing of the Pecos River located there) on a long-term basis, began as early as November 1826, when the cabo José Larrañaga and nine soldiers were ordered to proceed there and stay "until the receipt of new orders." There is no indication how long Larrañaga and his men stayed but the practice of stationing troops at San Miguel continued through the 1830s in response to numerous reports of Native American raids in the region. In late March of 1830, José Antonio Vizcarra, as military commander of the Santa Fe presidio, dispatched the alférez José Silva and twenty-seven men to San Miguel to establish an outpost at that location. Silva and his men departed Santa Fe on March 29, 1830, marched through Apache Canyon past Pecos to the settlement at El Gusano, and arrived at San Miguel del Bado on March 31.

Silva's report shows that they remained at San Miguel for three days with nothing significant to report. One can presume they spent this time unpacking their gear and setting up camp. On April 4, Silva began sending out scouting parties of nine men to search for locations where hostile raiding parties could hide and approach the communities without being spotted. The scouting parties rotated this duty every third day. On April 10, Silva received word from the local alcalde that seven men had been killed by Native Americans at a sheep camp near the Ancón de Felipe Sanches. Silva immediately sent a messenger to Santa Fe to report the incident and prepared to pursue the raiders and recover the bodies.

Silva, fifteen soldiers, and ten militiamen from San Miguel left the settlement on April 11 and reached Anton Chico that evening, where they encamped for the night. The following morning, they proceeded to Agua Negra, which they reached on the 13th, before arriving at the Ancón de Felipe Sanches. Silva and his patrol spent two days scouting the area in search of the bodies reportedly killed by raiding Native Americans but found only one body, and concluded that the report had been vastly exaggerated. Unable to do more, the troops returned to San Miguel on the afternoon of the 14th, arriving at their camp at three o'clock, the afternoon of the 16th.

For the next two weeks, Silva and his men settled into a camp routine of drills, inspections, and the rotating scouts that went out every third day. Silva remained with his men at San Miguel until April 31, when he received orders to turn over command of the post to his unnamed cabo and return to Santa Fe.

This troop presence at San Miguel apparently had a positive effect on hostilities in the region as reports of raids seem to have subsided during the subsequent weeks. However, raiding resumed toward the end of summer and a series of reports noted that the Pawnees had attacked Anton Chico in late August 1830 and killed one citizen. A troop of forty-two men pursued the raiders to the Rio Colorado but were unable to catch them. Subsequent raids prompted Governor José Antonio Chaves to recommend to his superiors in Chihuahua that a permanent outpost of thirty men be established at San Miguel to help protect the eastern frontier.

I have found no record that shows when the permanent outpost was officially established at San Miguel. By September 1832, however, solders were stationed there on at least a semi-permanent basis and correspondence and reports of the period begin to refer to families of the soldiers being there. Certainly, by November of 1832 correspondence of commanding officer José Antonio Vizcarra mentions official recruiting for the company at San Miguel del Bado. From 1832 until the US occupation in 1846, a company that numbered between twenty and thirty men and officers was stationed at San Miguel—making this community a key element in the tenuous defense of New Mexico's eastern frontier.

A Soldier's Career

More often than I like to admit, one gets sidetracked from research projects by a few words or lines in a document that have nothing to do with what one is looking for at that moment. This column is the result of one of those distractions—one which ended up becoming more and more interesting as I looked beyond the simple document that had initially drawn my attention.

While looking through microfilm of the Mexican Archives of New Mexico, my attention was drawn to a small piece of paper in the military records of the presidio company of Santa Fe. In the records of troop accounts there is a piece of paper no more than a quarter sheet in size dated April 12, 1834. It is a simple request by the cabo Antonio Sena for an advance of six pesos on his salary of twenty-five pesos a month so he could purchase some items for his wife, whom he noted had recently given birth. Blas de Hinojos, the company commander, approved the advance in the amount of five pesos and the account shows that Sena was given the cash that same day.

Curiosity about whether I could find a record of baptism for the child Sena alluded to in the request led me to a search through some of the records of the Archdiocese of Santa Fe for the period. I did not find the child's baptismal record, but in the process I found that Sena himself was baptized in Santa Fe on March 19, 1809. He was the son of José Manuel de Jesús Sena and María Josefa Madrid. His service record shows that on June 10, 1829, at the age of twenty, Sena entered military service with the presidio company of Santa Fe. He held the rank of soldado, or private, for little more than three and a half years

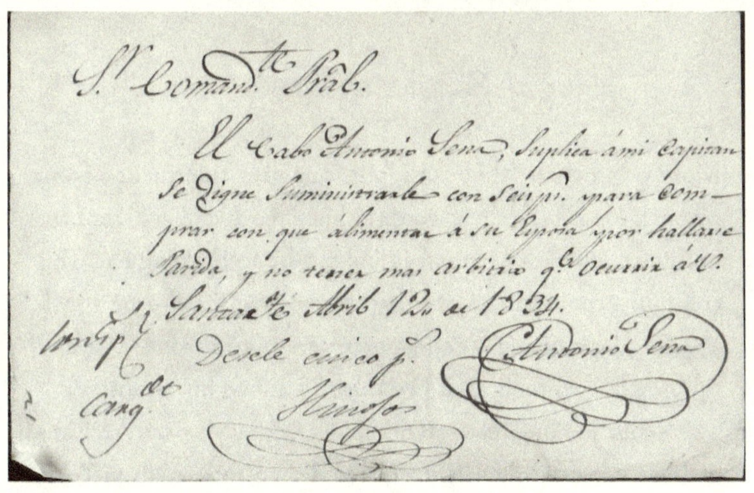

Sr. Comandte. Gral.

El Cabo Antonio Sena, Suplica á mi Capitan se digne Suministrarle con seis ps. para comprar con que alimentar á su Esposa por hallarse Parida, y no tener mas arbitrio qe. Ocurrir á V.

Santa Fe Abril 12 de 1834.

Desele cinco p.

Hinojos

Antonio Sena

Figure 13. Antonio Sena, request for funds, April 12, 1834. MANM: 1834 Military Records, Miscellaneous Receipts.

before being promoted to cabo in 1832. During this period he married María del Refugio Ortiz from Santa Cruz de la Cañada. I assume the child he referred to in his 1834 request was the result of his marriage to María del Refugio.

At the point that I found out this much of his personal life, I was once again drawn to his service record. Service records are one of the little-known treasures of our Mexican Archives of New Mexico. This collection contains thousands of records pertaining to individual soldiers who served in the military during New Mexico's Mexican period. As it turns out, the records pertaining to Antonio Sena are extraordinarily complete and tell us a lot, not only about the man, but also about that period of our history.

Some of the most interesting of Sena's records are the numerous hojas de servicio, the service records that detail his

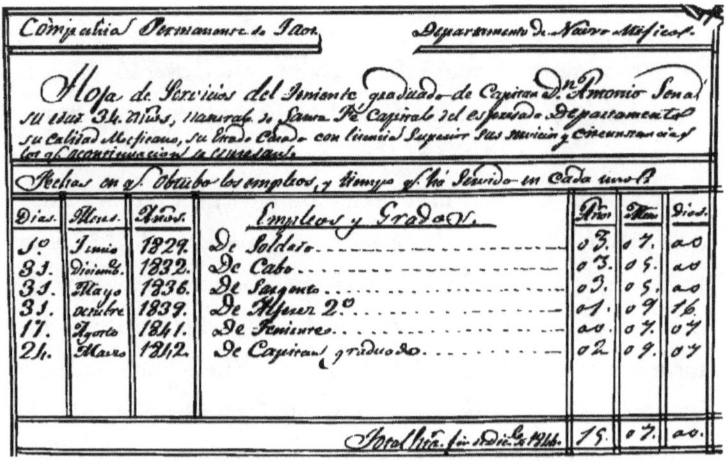

Compañía Permanente de Taos. — Departamento de Nuevo México.

Hoja de Servicios del Teniente graduado de Capitán D.n Antonio Sena, su edad 34 años, natural de Santa Fe capital del espresado Departamento, su calidad Mexicano, su Estado Casado con licencia Superior, sus servicios y circunstancias los q.e a continuación [illegible]

Fechas en q.e obtubo los empleos, y tiempo q.e ha servido en cada uno.

Dias.	Meses.	Años.	Empleos y Grados.	Años	Meses	Dias.
1.o	Junio	1829.	De Soldado	03.	07.	00
31.	Diciemb.e	1832.	De Cabo	03.	05.	00
31.	Mayo	1836.	De Sargento	03.	05.	00
31.	octubre	1839.	De Alferez 2.o	01.	09	16.
17.	Agosto	1841.	De Teniente	00.	07.	07
21.	Marzo	1842.	De Capitan graduado	02	09.	07
			Total hta. fin de Dic.e de 18[illegible]	15.	07.	00.

Figure 14. Antonio Sena, *hoja de servicios* (service record), 1842. MANM: Military Records, Service Records, Bado Company.

entire career from the time he enlisted in 1829 through his rise through the ranks of captain in 1842. These include his promotion to cabo in 1832, to sergeant in 1836, *alférez segundo* in 1839, *alférez primero* in 1841, and finally, to captain in 1842. They also show that he participated in at least three major Native American campaigns. The first of these occurred within four months of his enlistment while escorting the commercial caravan traveling from Santa Fe to the United States. On October 6, 1829, he took part in a skirmish with the Pawnees near the Cimarron River and took part in campaigns against the Navajos in 1834 and 1835.

Of special significance, however, was the part Sena took in two battles during the northern New Mexico insurrection known as the Revolt of 1837. Sergeant Sena was part of the small contingent of troops that accompanied Governor Albino Pérez from Santa Fe to suppress the rebellion centered around the communities of Santa Cruz and Chimayo. The reports indicate that Sena may have been captured by the rebels during a desperate battle with the "*Canaderos*" on August 8, 1837, but he was apparently released or escaped because he was with the forces commanded by Manuel Armijo, which crushed the insurrection in January 1838. One cannot help but wonder if his sense of duty to the Mexican Republic may have pitted him against some of his relatives on the battlefield. His wife, after all, was from Santa Cruz.

Sena's long military record, however, is crowned by his actions during the Texas invasion of New Mexico in 1841. In recognition of his service against the invading Texans, Manuel Armijo, his commanding officer and governor of New Mexico, recommended him for an "*escudo de honor*," an embroidered badge that was worn on the left sleeve of the uniform. This honor was granted to Sena by the president of the Republic of Mexico a few months later, along with his promotion to captain.

This brief look at the life of Antonio Sena shows his development from a raw recruit to a professional soldier and patriot of the Mexican Republic. He had come a long way since his enlistment in 1829 and that day in 1834 when his concern for the welfare of his wife had prompted him to request an advance on his salary. It was that simple piece of paper, that voice from the past, that had drawn my attention to begin with.

A War Widow's Petition for Pension, 1835

Raids on New Mexico's towns and pueblos by the Comanches, Navajos, Apaches, and Utes were a constant threat to the peace and prosperity of the province throughout the Spanish and Mexican eras. The 1830s were a period of almost constant warfare. Hundreds of documents in our Mexican Archives of New Mexico provide details of the human tragedies and material costs behind this most difficult period of our history.

Many of these documents describe Navajo raids and the subsequent military campaigns against the Navajos between 1836 and 1839, beginning early in the governorship of Albino Pérez. While the Navajo raids that took place earlier in that decade are not as well documented, there is among these a fascinating series of letters that drew my attention because they were written in support of a widow's petition for a pension due to the death of her husband, a casualty of a February 1835 Navajo campaign.

Pensions for widows and orphans of military personnel killed in the line of duty during New Mexico's Spanish era were featured in a column published in 2001. At that time, I emphasized the pensions granted to María Ignacia Bernal, widow of Vicente Troncoso, who died while on duty in 1792, and to María Dolores, daughter of Alejandro Ortiz, who was killed during an Apache campaign in 1789. In late 1820, a viceregal order had detailed the process by which pensions were to be paid to families of soldiers killed in actions of war, so it is possible the practice was in place during the Mexican period.

In a document dated May 30, 1835, Juan Rafael Ortiz, acting on behalf of María Josefa Gallego (also spelled Gallegos) de Baca, a resident of Peña Blanca, submitted a petition in which she identified herself as the widow of the late Juan Antonio Baca, formerly the constitutional alcalde of the jurisdiction of Cochiti, who had given his life in service to his country. "Finding myself surrounded by a large family and reduced to the most lamentable state of misery," her petition noted, "for the reasons I shall demonstrate, I find it necessary to place myself at the mercy of your Excellency, begging that you may make my condition known to the Supreme Government, who may justly remediate my needs."

Doña María then proceeded to explain that despite the loss of all their assets to the incessant raids and incursions of enemy tribes, her husband accepted the challenge of marching against the Apache and Navajo tribes whenever he was called to do so. Most recently he joined a campaign against the Navajos under the command of Captains Blas Hinojos and Francisco Sarracino, during which he was killed.

The petition was accompanied by seven supporting documents submitted by a "who's who" of Mexican officialdom, including former governor Francisco Sarracino, district judge Santiago Abreu, the constitutional alcalde of Santa Fe, Juan Doroteo Pino, administrator of revenues Ramon Abreu, first vocal of the Territorial Diputación Juan Rafael Ortiz, and principal clerk and auditor Vicente Sanches Vergara. These documents show that Baca was wounded in a battle with the Navajos on February 28, 1835, and died of his wounds two days later. Every letter emphasized Baca's valor and well-known service to his country. He was, noted Santiago Abreu, "without a doubt, a true New Mexican Hero."

On June 1, 1835, Governor Albino Pérez acknowledged receipt of the petition and accompanying documents and noted that it appeared to him that the late Juan Antonio Baca, "was a citizen who sacrificed himself in service to his country, and left behind a large and impoverished family which deserved due consideration of the Supreme Government." Governor Pérez apparently looked into the matter before forwarding the petition to Mexico and sought confirmation that doña Maria was the legitimate widow of her deceased husband. In a formal and tersely worded letter dated July 20, 1836 (more than a year after she had submitted the petition), Fray Mariano José Sánchez Vergara, pastor for the missions of San Felipe, Santa Ana, Zia, Jemez, and Cochiti, certified he had carefully reviewed the marriage register at San Felipe but did not find an entry regarding the marriage of the late don Juan Antonio Cabesa de Baca and doña Josefa Gallegos y Chaves. He acknowledged that the marriage may have been recorded at another mission but tersely noted that having personally known the parents, grandparents, and godparents of the couple, "if they had not been legitimately married, the parents would never have consented . . . for them to establish a separate household close by and procreate children in such a public manner."

Despite the support of these prominent officials and apparent need of doña María and her impoverished family, which consisted of thirteen children, eight of them still quite young, it appears the petition and its supporting documents were never forwarded to the central government in Mexico and if it was, there is no indication that any action was ever taken. Regardless, these voices from the past provide a human face to one of the personal tragedies that befell our ancestors and furnish us with valuable details of their lives.

CHAPTER THREE

The Navajo Campaign of 1836

Relations with hostile frontier tribes nearly destroyed New Mexico during the Mexican period. The civil and military records in the Spanish and Mexican Archives of New Mexico reveal a tragic and seemingly endless cycle of raids, retaliatory campaigns, peace negotiations, and broken treaties. This cycle of hostilities can be best exemplified by the records of the Navajo campaigns of 1836 through 1838. The 1836 campaign records also provide a useful, although incomplete list of militia assigned to the campaign from various jurisdictions in New Mexico.

The process of planning for and organizing the 1836 Navajo campaign began early during the administration of Governor Albino Pérez. On February 19, 1836, Pérez, as gefe politico y military chief, issued a circular to the alcaldes throughout the territory advising that his ongoing efforts to achieve a lasting peace with the Navajos had failed. The treaty negotiated with them at San Miguel del Bado in 1835 had quickly fallen apart and the tribe, or at least certain elements of them, had already resumed raiding frontier communities. Consequently, he authorized all jurisdictions to pursue and prosecute any such raiders without mercy and by whatever means possible and necessary. He also ordered local authorities to conduct musters of men eligible for militia service every fifteen days and keep all weapons and ammunition ready to defend the frontier.

Navajo raids continued throughout the spring of 1836. On June 1, 1836, Pérez advised all the alcaldes to prepare lists of their best men and that he would personally lead a campaign against the Navajos in early September. On July 21, he issued specific campaign orders and instructions to José Francisco Vigil, commander of the volunteers from the northern New Mexico jurisdictions of San Juan de Los Caballeros, Taos, Ojo Caliente, Abiquiú, Trampas, and Santa Clara. Pérez also reminded Vigil that the Navajo chiefs who had managed to keep the peace were not to be disturbed during this campaign and if possible, their help utilized. Included in these documents are the lists of men designated for the campaign from these communities.

These extant lists constitute only a small portion of the musters prepared for the campaign. On August 24, 1836, when Governor Pérez issued his final orders for the campaign, he estimated two thousand men would participate. When the campaign kicked off on September 12, Pérez's reports expressed disappointment at the smaller number that showed up, but he did not specify a final count. Even if all the men listed in the extant musters reported for duty, it is clear these seven hundred or so individuals constituted less than half of those expected to report. In addition to those who did not report for duty, a number of exemptions were allowed. Militia regulations of the time allowed those who were too elderly or ill to participate to name a competent substitute, as long as the person named was mounted and well armed.

The campaign itself was organized into three divisions commanded by tenientes José Caballero, Francisco Mares, and José Silva. During the nearly six weeks the expedition was in the field, twenty Navajos were reported killed or taken captive, more than two thousand livestock captured, and one New Mexican captive recovered. In all the military operations, only one New Mexican casualty was reported. On October 15, Francisco García died at Zuni, a victim of the cold temperatures and rigors of the campaign. García, the lieutenants José Caballero and José Silva, alférez Esquipula Caballero, Francisco Martines, Rafael Tapia and Ramon Baca, and sergeants José Ortega, Baltasar Sandoval, José Larrañaga, and Francisco Campos were commended by Pérez for serving "with the honor of true soldiers, each carrying out his duty to my great satisfaction."

The campaign, however, failed to achieve its principal goal—to deal the Navajos a decisive blow and force them to seek peace. Some Navajo envoys did come to Santa Fe to discuss terms of a lasting peace, but the negotiations broke down and the raiding soon resumed. By November 20, Pérez was already planning another more ambitious campaign to be carried out in late December 1836 through January 1837. In his report to the comandante general in Chihuahua, Pérez indicated he expected to deliver a decisive blow to the Navajos when they least expected it—in the midst of winter. "I will not accept peace until I have punished them severely," he wrote, "in order to make them understand that while New Mexicans are humble in peace, they can enthusiastically wage war on their enemies."

The Navajo Campaign of 1836–1837

Among the seemingly endless stories contained within the Spanish and Mexican Archives of New Mexico are the numerous reports of campaigns against the tribes that raided settlements along New Mexico's vast frontier. The previous chapter featured the military campaign conducted against the Navajos by Governor

Albino Pérez in the summer of 1836. This article continues with a review of the subsequent campaigns Pérez organized against the Navajos in the winter of 1836–1837.

On November 1, 1836, Governor Pérez submitted a report to the comandante general in Chihuahua detailing his recently concluded summer campaign against the Navajos in western New Mexico. Pérez felt that the campaign, which lasted nearly six weeks, had inflicted enough casualties and damage to the various Navajo settlements, or rancherías, that they would be unable to muster any effective raiding forces for some time to come.

Pérez was wrong. Despite his enthusiastic prediction, the Navajos apparently resumed raiding almost immediately and by late November 1836, the governor was busy organizing another campaign. Despite a general lack of resources available to finance and equip a large military force, he hoped to gather at least one thousand militia for the campaign. His plan was to deliver a decisive blow when the Navajos least expected it—in the winter.

Pérez left Santa Fe on December 9, 1836, and marched to the western New Mexico settlement of Cubero, where he was joined by the forces that had been ordered to gather there from throughout the territory. The force of 750 men who had answered the muster at Cubero was smaller than Pérez hoped, but still significant under the circumstances. He divided the men into five companies. The first was placed under command of Julian Tenorio of Albuquerque; the second under Fernando Aragón of Sandia; the third under José Martínez of Bernalillo; the fourth under José Francisco Vigil of San Juan; and the fifth under José Gonzales of Taos (likely the same José Gonzales who one year later was named governor following Governor Pérez's assassination).

The expedition left Cubero on December 17, arriving at Zuni on the 24th. From Zuni several operations were directed into the Navajo country in which several rancherías were destroyed, prisoners taken, and several thousand livestock captured. In the various actions, Pérez reported that two of his citizen soldiers were wounded. One of these men, José Sebastián, later died.

By January 12, 1837, the expedition was sweeping toward the Cañon de Chelly in eastern Arizona, where Pérez felt they could deliver a decisive military blow to the Navajos. That night, however, a severe snowstorm brought the campaign to an abrupt halt. When the snow lifted, freezing temperatures killed several livestock. Fearing they would lose the horses and pack animals, the commanders reluctantly decided to break off the expedition and began their difficult trek back to the warmth and comfort of their homes.

While the details of the military aspects of this campaign are very interesting, the extraordinary hardships suffered by the troops constituted an important element of the expedition. Governor Pérez's report makes it clear that much of the campaign was waged in extremely cold weather and deep snows. Between Cubero and Zuni, the horses were breaking trail in snow up to their chests so that the pack animals and the infantry could pass. During the action in which José Sebastián was killed, fifty-four men suffered from varying degrees of frostbite. Juan Lueras, for example, lost two fingers of his left hand, and in another action, 140 of the men suffered frostbite of their hands and feet, while another lost an ear and three toes.

The hardships endured by these citizen militia was exceeded only by the suffering of the Navajos. In addition to the Navajos killed and captured, Governor Pérez reported that numerous rancherías had been dispersed, depriving them of shelter and exposing them to the weather. He felt that more Navajos had died because of this subsequent exposure than from the armed encounters of the campaign itself.

The governor concluded that although the campaign had failed to completely defeat the Navajos and eliminate them as a threat to frontier settlements, their efforts had partially succeeded. He noted that two days after he arrived in Santa Fe, four Navajo representatives came into the city seeking peace negotiations. If these had succeeded in achieving even a short respite of hostilities, the suffering on both sides during the expeditions of 1836–1837 might not have been in vain.

The Navajo Campaigns of 1838–1839

As we have seen in the previous two chapters, the Navajo campaigns of 1836 and 1837 conducted by Governor Albino Pérez did nothing to achieve a lasting peace or discourage the Navajos from raiding communities along New Mexico's frontier. Sporadic raiding continued through the winter and spring of 1837. However, as Pérez contemplated another concerted campaign against the Navajos, New Mexico was thrown into the turmoil of the "Revolt of 1837," which resulted in the death of Governor Pérez and several officials of his administration. It is possible the physical and financial hardships imposed on

New Mexico's citizen soldiers by the preceding campaigns were a significant factor in the animosity and opposition that developed against the Pérez administration in the spring of 1837 and the subsequent insurrection.

New Mexico was unable to muster the resources to respond to the Navajo raids that continued throughout 1837 and 1838. It was late summer 1838 before Manuel Armijo, who had assumed the role of governor following Pérez's assassination, could muster sufficient presidio and militia forces to respond effectively to raiding by hostiles. By late spring 1838, New Mexico military forces had been reinforced by the Mexican squadron from Vera Cruz that had been sent to assist in suppressing the 1837 insurrection. A force of 978 men, consisting of militia and 130 soldiers of the Santa Fe presidio and Vera Cruz squadrons, left Jémez on or about September 13, 1838. For nearly three weeks, these men conducted operations south to the Gila, where they concluded the campaign with a pitched battle with the Navajos and some allied Apaches.

Governor Armijo's memorandum of November 6, 1838, ordered the following statement be inserted into the service records of the officers and men who participated in the recently concluded campaign. The statement effectively provides an official summary of what the campaign accomplished. Each entry noted that the particular officer or soldier had participated in the campaign:

> . . . during the months of September and October of 1838, achieved the death of 78 warriors, imprisonment of 56 individuals of both sexes, the rescue of one of our captives, capture of

> 226 horses and mules (*vestias*), 2060 sheep, 160 *gamusas* (finely tanned hides) six serapes, all their personal property as well as destroyed or captured 1600 *costales* (sacks) of corn.

Once again, the campaign brought about no lasting respite from Navajo raids. By early December 1838, another campaign had been organized. On December 9 of that year, expedition commander Pedro León Luján departed Abiquiú with fourteen soldiers of the Santa Fe *presidio* and 248 militia from the northern New Mexico communities of Abiquiú, Santa Cruz de la Cañada, Chama (today's Chamita, or possibly, Hernández), Taos, Ojo Caliente, San Juan, San Yldefonso, Trampas, and Rito Colorado. Luján's journal of the campaign indicates that they were in the field more than two weeks and had at least one major clash with the Navajos on December 21.

In the early spring of 1839, several of the principal Navajo chiefs, or capitancillos, as they were often called, sent representatives to the Pueblo of Jémez to ask the Mexican government for a meeting to consider a negotiated peace. The correspondence regarding initial arrangements for such a meeting identified six principal Navajo chiefs among those seeking peace negotiations—Narbona, Chato (Flat-Nose), Calletano, el Barbón (the Bearded One), el Guero (the Blond One), and Facundo.

The following weeks witnessed a frenzied exchange of letters and orders regarding the proposed negotiations. Governor Armijo expressed a guarded optimism when he reported to his superiors in Chihuahua that the successful blows they had administered to the Navajos in recent years may have prompted the chiefs to seek peace. As an act of good faith, he suspended all planned actions against them, but added that if the Navajos did not come to negotiate a treaty as promised, he would conduct another campaign against them as soon as the subsequent American trading caravan arrived and funds became available.

In late April, Armijo began issuing orders designed to guarantee protection for the Navajo envoys and to demonstrate his good faith toward the impending negotiations. He ordered that when Navajo envoys or representatives were encountered, they were to be well treated and escorted to Jémez where the negotiations were to be held. By April 26, several Navajos had arrived at Jémez and two of these were selected to travel to Santa Fe and meet with Governor Armijo. Details of their meeting with Armijo are not extant, but Calletano, one of the capitancillos mentioned earlier, may have been one of the initial envoys because one report noted that "his people" could be in Santa Fe to meet on May 27 or 28. As we shall see in our next chapter, the subsequent peace negotiations held at the Pueblo of Jémez accomplished little. Within weeks, the raiding resumed and another seemingly endless cycle of retaliation, negotiations, and raiding began anew.

The Navajo Peace Treaty of 1839

Previous chapters reviewed the results of the Mexican government's campaigns against the Navajos in the late 1830s and Governor Manuel Armijo's subsequent efforts to negotiate a lasting peace treaty with the tribe. In late June 1839, Governor Armijo advised local officials that he planned to meet with

Navajo leaders at the Pueblo of Jémez on July 14 to conduct peace negotiations, and that he expected to be escorted to the meeting by the "most utilitarian and respectable persons" of the territory. Juan Andres Archuleta, prefect of New Mexico's northern district, named a company of fifty men from Abiquiú and El Rito under command of Captain Pedro León Luján and ordered them to meet Governor Armijo at Jémez. Antonio Sandoval, prefect of the rio abajo, or southern district, also named thirty of his district's most prominent citizens and proceeded to the meeting site. The order from Armijo specified that the representatives from southern New Mexico should include "the Chaves, Oteros and Pereas" because they would be among those who would benefit most from successful peace negotiations, no doubt because their flocks were primary targets of Navajo raids.

The list of those who attended the peace negotiations has not survived, but the meeting was held as scheduled on July 15, 1839. A draft of the treaty is found in the Governor's Papers of the Mexican Archives of New Mexico. According to Governor Armijo's report to his superiors in Mexico, the treaty consisted of seven principal sections:

1. That there would be peace and commerce between Navajos and the citizens of New Mexico, Chihuahua, and Sonora.
2. To demonstrate their good faith, the Navajo chiefs agreed to turn over all the Mexican captives they had because these had been taken forcibly from the camps where they were watching their livestock. The Navajo captives held by the New Mexicans could remain

"amongst us" because they were acquired by means of "honorable warfare and purchase."

3. The principal Navajo leaders agreed to do everything in their power to see that their people would not disturb the peace and order of the citizens of New Mexico.
4. All commerce within the Department was to be regulated in the same manner as it was before the current outbreak of hostilities.
5. The Navajos agreed to turn over to Mexican authorities any Navajo who killed a herder for proper punishment by Mexican authorities. If a Navajo was killed, the herder would pay his family the customary price and be punished according to the law.
6. If a Navajo captive held by New Mexicans escaped his captors and returned to Navajo territory, he would remain free.
7. If a common enemy threatened an invasion, each side was obligated to resist the invasion or at least warn the other by sending word to the frontier at Cebolleta or Jémez.

Within weeks, copies of the treaty were being circulated throughout New Mexico. However, the expected long-sought peace did not materialize. By the middle of September, northern prefect Juan Andres Archuleta was advising local officials in his jurisdiction that the Navajo chief Narbona had informed authorities at Jémez that "his countrymen" had declared a state of war with the Mexicans. A party of two hundred warriors was expected to raid the Rio Puerco very soon. Subsequent reports show that the peace treaty of July 15 was never seriously implemented. It is not clear which of the treaty conditions may have prompted either of the parties to resume hostilities, but on October 1, 1839, less than three months after the treaty at the Pueblo of Jemez was negotiated, Governor Armijo sent out notice that war with the Navajos had been officially renewed and to begin preparations for a campaign against them.

On October 18, 1839, Juan Andres Archuleta reported that a force consisting of 253 cavalry and 232 infantry had been organized and placed in the field. Two hundred twenty-eight of the men carried firearms and the remainder were equipped with the principal militia armaments of the period: bows, arrows, and lances. The force was composed entirely from the following northern New Mexico communities:

Santa Fe: 7
San Miguel del Bado: 22
San Juan: 71
Trampas: 48
San Fernando de Taos: 47
Rito: 46
Santa Clara: 59
Ranchos de Taos: 66
Abiquiú: 57
Santa Cruz de la Cañada: 66

The report and journal of operations of this latest Navajo campaign shows that these men were in the field for nearly two months.

This newest outbreak of hostilities led to the usual tragedies. As Archuleta's October–December 1839 campaign against the Navajos wound down, the Navajos took the offensive and conducted a raid on the Belen region in which sixteen woodcutters were killed. The raids prompted another round of hostilities that finally wound down in early 1840. At that time, the Navajos again sent emissaries to discuss yet another peace treaty. However, these efforts also came to naught. By late September 1840, Governor Armijo had organized another campaign, opening another chapter in the tragic and seemly endless cycle of war with the Navajos that continued even into the first decades of New Mexico's territorial period.

A Massacre in the *Rio Abajo*

One of the most fascinating and informative long-term research projects related to New Mexico's history has been conducted by Dr. Oswald Baca of Tomé. Dr. Baca has painstakingly analyzed the burial records of the southern New Mexico parish of Belen and extracted the causes of death that parish priests often entered in the burial records. Among them are several dozen people who are listed as having been killed by Apaches, Navajos, and other raiders identified only as "Enemies."

Some years ago, Dr. Baca mentioned a series of sixteen burials performed at Belen by Father Rafael Ortiz on December 4, 1839. All sixteen burials have the same entry, which notes that each received ecclesiastical burial but not the last rites of the Church because they were "killed by the enemy Navajo." These

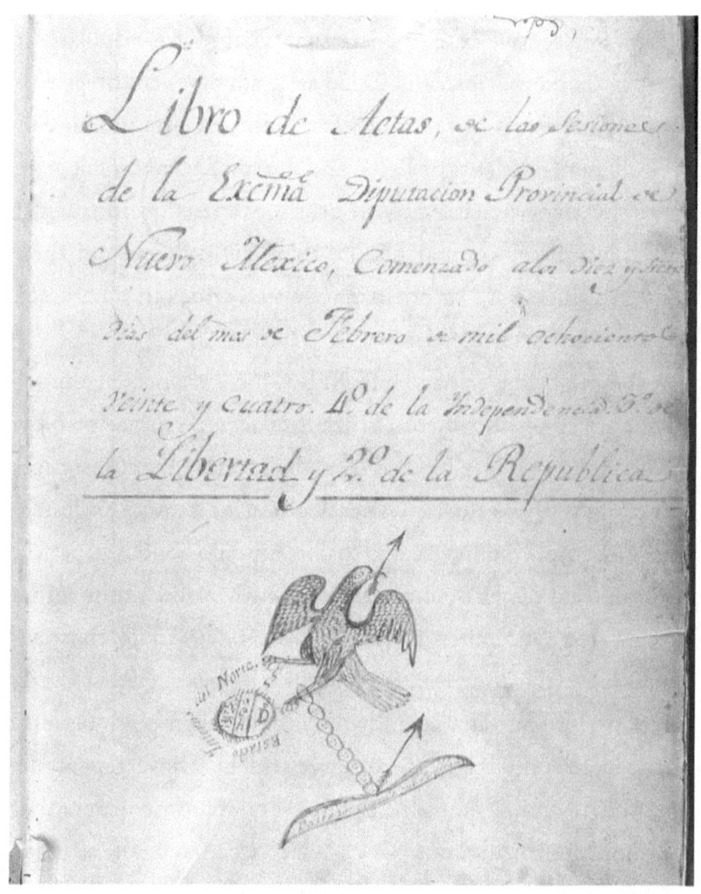

Figure 15. The Mexican Eagle depicted on the opening page of the New Mexico *diputación* journal of proceedings illustrates two issues that inhibited the territory's prosperity—its administrative attachment to the states of Durango and Chihuahua, and the constant state of war with the region's tribes. Note the wording within the bow, "¿Barbaros cuando me sueltan?" (Barbarians, when will you release me?). MANM: Legislative Records, Journal of the Diputación Provincial and Diputación Territorial, 1824–1828.

sixteen consecutive entries document what may be the largest number of New Mexicans killed in a single encounter with Native Americans in the nineteenth century. The individuals were all men, residents of Belen and nearby Sausal. What were the circumstances that led to the deaths of so many individuals? Was it a military campaign? Did they die in defense of their homes during a raid by one of the several tribes that harassed these frontier settlements?

We might never have known but for a chance encounter with a series of documents in the Mexican Archives of New Mexico that manages to shed some light on the circumstances surrounding these burials. These consist of a series of letters from Governor Manuel Armijo to don Antonio Sandoval, prefect of the second district (southern) of New Mexico. In the initial letter, dated December 10, 1839, Governor Armijo chastises Sandoval for "the disgraceful events which have occurred in several places under your charge and which have taken place because of the persistent failure to observe orders I have repeatedly sent you." Armijo reminded Sandoval of standing orders that communities throughout New Mexico were to be on alert for the hostile tribes that constantly raided along the frontier. He told Sandoval to remind local authorities in the region that no one was to be allowed to graze their livestock on *la otra banda,* the other bank of the river. The letter does not specify if that meant the west side of the Rio Grande or the Rio Puerco, which is located further west. He also ordered that the "*leñeros,*" woodcutters of the region, were to confine their activities to the hills and bosques (wooded areas along rivers) on the east side of this unnamed river.

Then the letter finally gets to the point. Armijo states that by having allowed a group of leñeros to cross the river in violation of these orders, Juan Antonio Torres, the justice of the peace from Belen, had personally caused the deaths of the sixteen men. He ordered Sandoval to immediately arrest Torres and send him to Santa Fe to account for his actions.

Two weeks later, Armijo again wrote to Sandoval and informed him that Torres was being released and exonerated of any responsibility in the deaths of the sixteen men. Instead, he noted that the *amos*, the masters of the individuals killed, were to be held personally responsible. It was they who had ordered their *mosos* (servants), to cut wood on the west side of the river and had sent a party that was poorly armed and too small to effectively defend themselves. They also apparently did so without Torres's knowledge or permission. Armijo sent Sandoval a list of the individuals he identified as responsible for these actions and ordered him to fine each of them twelve pesos and distribute the money among the widows and families of those who had been killed. The fines were to be imposed without exception and the individuals on the list were also to pay for the burials and any other expenses incurred by Father Ortiz. It is unfortunate that the list Armijo says he sent has not survived. It would have been interesting to see what names were on it, and to see if they are the same as those normally associated as the *patrones* (bosses) of the rio abajo.

While these letters shed some light on the circumstances that led to the deaths of the sixteen men buried at Belen on December 4, 1839, one wonders how far twelve pesos went in those days. One wonders whether the families of the men buried that sad day—Francisco Padilla, Toribio Pino, Jesús Rael, Juan Pino, José Rafael Chaves and his brother José Gabriel, Juan and Rafael Alderete, Matias Mireles, Jesús María Ribera, José María Montoya, Francisco Jaramillo, José Antonio Benavides, Juan José Jaramillo, José María Sanches, and Juan Belasques—felt it was just compensation for the tragic loss they had incurred.

Governor Manuel Armijo's Medal of Honor

The Albuquerque Museum has in its collections a full-length color portrait of Governor Manuel Armijo in a formal military uniform, wearing a sword, a plumed hat, and a medal adorning the left side of his chest. The portrait was painted by the itinerary artist Alfred S. Waugh in June 1846. Waugh described the painting as "a cabinet size picture, a full-length figure in full uniform, with the cross of honor given by Santa Anna, on his breast, and the sword, presented by the people of Chihuahua, at his side."

There are two extant versions of the Armijo portrait Waugh described: the full-length version held by the Albuquerque Museum, and the second, a half-length likeness currently on display at the New Mexico History Museum in Santa Fe. While the paintings themselves are of interest, what drew my attention was the "cross of honor" noted by Waugh. Neither painting shows the medal in any detail, causing one to wonder what it actually looked like, but more importantly, why and when Governor Armijo was awarded this distinctive decoration.

A "Voices From the Past" column on the portrait and medal was first published in August 2002, but at that time there were

Figure 16. Governor Manuel Armijo portrait. Ralph Emerson Twitchell, *The History of the Military Occupation of the Territory of New Mexico from 1846 to 1851* (Rio Grande Press, Inc., 1963), 55.

many unanswered questions about the medal, which prompted my long-time colleague and friend Charles Martínez and myself to look deeper into the history behind the painting and Armijo's medal. What we found indicates that this was an important military decoration awarded by the Mexican government to one of New Mexico history's most important and influential people. The research resulted in a full-length article published in *Wagon Tracks*, the journal of the Santa Fe Trail Association in August of 2023. This chapter is a condensed version of the *Wagon Tracks* article and not the original 2002 "Voices Form the Past" column.

One of the defining moments of New Mexico's short tenure as a territory of the Mexican Republic came in 1841. That year, Texas president Mirabeau B. Lamar sent an armed force known as the Texas-Santa Fe Expedition to New Mexico in hopes of opening trade between the Texas capital in Austin and Santa Fe, but also expected to exercise the Texans' claim that the Rio Grande was their western border and encourage New Mexico to become part of the Texan Republic. The expedition under General Hugh McLeod, however, failed miserably for a number of reasons. By the time the Texans arrived at the settlements along New Mexico's eastern frontier, they were in no condition to resist and were easily captured by Governor Manuel Armijo's forces. By October 1841, McLeod and his men had been captured and were being escorted to Paso del Norte by Captain Damaso Salazar and a contingent of presidio troops and militia.

The news of Armijo's capture of the Texans was quickly hailed as a great victory, not only for New Mexico, but for a beleaguered Mexican nation. A circular issued at Paso del Norte on September 28, 1841, joyfully trumpeted the capture and defeat of the Texans. "Viva la Patria," it announced, "Los tejanos han sido vencidos" (The Texans have been defeated).

Capture of the Texans provided a great lift for the morale of the Mexican Republic and by December 1841, the Mexican government announced that Governor Armijo and officers of the contingent that had captured the Texans would be awarded *una cruz de honor* (a cross of honor) for their service. Armijo received his personal cruz de honor on January 7, 1846. When he acknowledged receipt of the medal, Governor Armijo noted that the box it had come in was damaged and that one of the jewels had come loose, but he had it in hand along with a length of green ribbon (*cinta verde*) that had accompanied the medal.

The official notice or certificate that likely accompanied Armijo's medal has eluded discovery, but we do have examples of the certificate that accompanied the award issued to several officers and militia who had distinguished themselves during the Texas campaign. An example of this certificate is a "Diploma" issued to Captain Guadalupe Miranda dated December 21, 1841. The certificate notes that the Mexican Congress had in 1840 authorized a cruz de honor for the men who served in "defense of the integrity of the National Territory" and awards "the citizen Guadalupe Miranda, Captain of army auxiliaries, for having concurred in the New Mexico campaign against the Texan adventurers in 1841, [an] escudo de honor for his service." It is important to note that although the certificate is clearly labeled as a "Diploma de la Cruz de Honor," the text substitutes the term *escudo*—an embroidered badge or patch that was to be worn on the left sleeve of the uniform—in place of the cruz de honor.

An identical "Diploma" was issued to Captain of Rural Militia Diego Archuleta on the same date. Archuleta's certificate is reproduced by Ralph Emerson Twitchell in his book on the military occupation of New Mexico. Twitchell describes Archuleta's decoration as a "golden Cross of Honor," suggesting it may have been similar to the one awarded to Governor Armijo. The Diploma, however, clearly describes the award as an escudo to be worn on the left sleeve.

Coauthor Charles Martínez has delved deeply into the service records of the Mexican Archives of New Mexico and identified the following individuals who received the same escudo de honor as Guadalupe Miranda:

Commandant of the Graduate Squadron and Captain of the Rural Militia Diego Archuleta
Commandant of the Superior Squadron and Captain of the Rural Militia Pascual Martínez
Lieutenant Colonel José Silva
Lieutenant Colonel Francisco Martínez
Captain Tomas Martínez
Captain Donaciano Vigil
Captain Antonio Sena
Captain of Auxiliaries Guadalupe Miranda
Lieutenant Tomas Armijo
Lieutenant Manuel Ramírez
Lieutenant Francisco Campos
Lieutenant Pablo Domínguez
Alférez (Ensign) Juan López
Alférez José Dolores Tafoya

Sergeant Francisco de la Peña
Sergeant Lorenzo Tafoya
Sergeant Ramón López
Sergeant José Tenorio
Sergeant Pedro Sandoval
Antonio Chávez
Ramon Martín
Ramon Sena
Juan Urioste
José Sánchez
José Sena

None of our research to date confirmed what Governor Armijo's cruz de honor looks like. Neither painting has much detail, but close examination of the full-length Armijo portrait suggests his "cruz de honor" has six green jewels along the outer edge. Considering Armijo's report that one of the jewels had come loose when he received it, Armijo's medal was a unique, singular award.

Governor Armijo's medal of honor and none of the escudos awarded to more than two dozen presidio troops and militia forces have surfaced. One can wonder if all these symbols of New Mexico's 1841 triumph over the Texans have disappeared. Or is it possible that some families still retain these unique artifacts, unaware of what they are and of the honor bestowed on their patriotic ancestors. Is an unidentified example or two sitting in storage at a museum, its significance unknown? Maybe one will surface in the future, and we can acknowledge and honor the service these men did for their country.

CHAPTER THREE

An Unexpected Treasure

During the three decades in which "Voices From the Past" has been published, I have encountered very few personal letters among the thousands of documents I have reviewed from our Spanish- and Mexican-era archives. Most correspondence received by government officials regards complaints about the loss of property, appeals of judicial decisions, and issues with or complaints about the church or government officials. These include numerous appeals from distraught parents asking for their sons to be exempted from militia service. While these can be considered personal, none that I can recall were from a wife to a husband who had been called to service during a military campaign.

However, I can now say that I found one—in a most unexpected place. While reviewing the Mexican Archives of New Mexico militia records associated with the 1841 campaign against the Texans, I came across a letter written by an obviously concerned wife to her husband, who had been called to serve in this brief but important event in New Mexico history. The heartfelt letter, dated September 24, 1841, is only a few lines long and is addressed to Sergeant Lorenzo Tafoya. The following is the full text in Spanish with some contemporary punctuation, capitalization, and accents added that were typically absent in the correspondence of the time:

> Estimado esposo. Logro esta ocación para saludarte en unión de tu hijita quien llora mucho por ti. Hasta ahora no tenemos

> novedad. La Francisca te saluda mucho. Dios guarde tu vida muchos años. Tu esposa, Ana Maria Rael
>
> Esteemed husband. I take this occasion to greet you in union with your young daughter who cries constantly for you. As of now we have no news. Francisca sends her sincere regards. God guard you many years. Your wife, Ana María Rael.

The letter takes up less than a quarter of a sheet of paper, which, when folded, would have made a neat, self-contained envelope, which was typical of the way letters of the era were mailed. The text makes it clear that Ana María Rael was literate. It was not signed with a cross (+), and the writing and signature appear to be her own. In the initial "Voices From the Past" column I suggested that her husband, Sergeant Tafoya, was also literate, and it is their literacy that may explain why this simple letter survived among the dozens of lists, orders, and other official military correspondence of that time. I later learned, however, that Tafoya's service record specifically states that he could not read or write.

We have no clue as to how the letter was delivered to Tafoya. Everything I have learned about the mail for that period indicates that it was generally undependable and that during September of 1841, things were likely downright chaotic in the midst of the frenetic activity and preparations being made to counter the threat posed by the Texan expedition. It is likely that couriers were going back and forth from Santa Fe to San Miguel del Bado, Las Vegas, Anton Chico, or wherever the troops were located

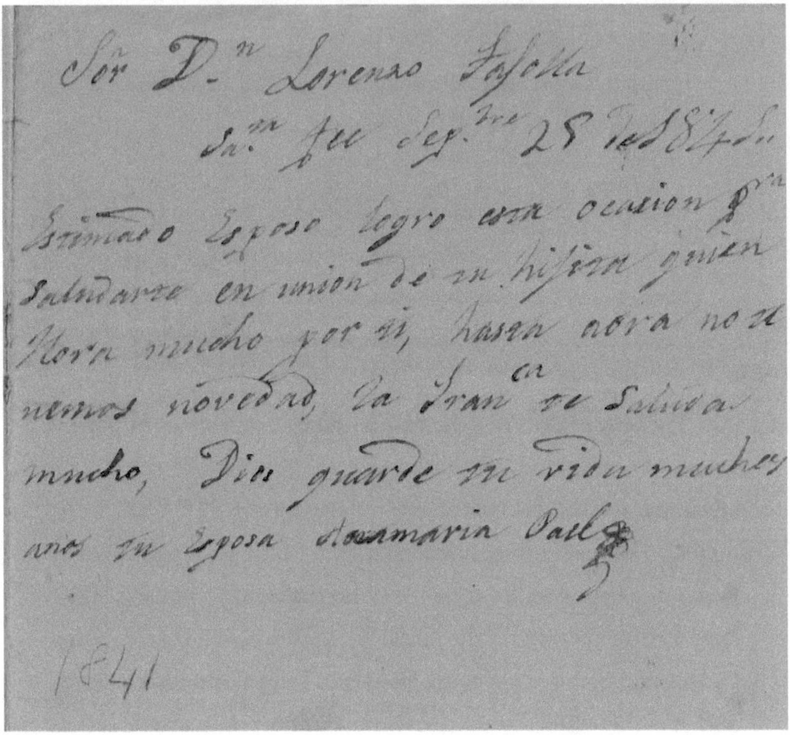

Figure 17. Letter, Ana María Rael to Lorenzo Tafoya, September 25, 1841. MANM: 1841 Military Records, Militia.

at the moment, and Ana María could have entrusted the letter to one of Tafoya's fellow soldiers.

Governor Manuel Armijo had received warning of the impending invasion from Texas as early as late fall of 1838 and had ample time to prepare. Administrative, military, and financial records of that period describe preparations made to organize the militia and provide food, uniforms, arms, ammunition, mounts, and the myriad supplies that a force of several hundred men needed to function. And of course, someone had to do the paperwork that accounted for all this.

This is where Ana María's letter comes in. Sergeant Tafoya had apparently been given the responsibility of delivering and distributing rams to feed the militia and troops, and lacking paper with which to make his reports, someone utilized the blank side of his wife's letter to prepare an account of the sheep Tafoya distributed to the troops and captured Texans over the course of several days.

The report, which was probably prepared in early October, is unsigned and possibly incomplete. It has the heading "List of the rams that the Sergeant Lorenzo Tafoya has distributed to date" and shows that between September 20 and 28, Tafoya distributed two hundred twenty-seven rams for *socorro* (rations) of the troops and captured Texans. These include distribution to several individuals who are listed by name—Mariano García, Antonio Sena, José Antonio Ulibarri, José Ensiñas, and military commander Lieutenant Colonel Juan Andres Archuleta, as well as to larger groups of militia and regular troops.

Despite his illiteracy, Tafoya had a distinguished military career. A native of Santa Fe, he enlisted as a soldier in the Santa Fe presidio in 1823, was promoted to the rank of cabo in 1828, and held that position until his promotion to sergeant in September 1841. For his service in the campaign against the Texans he was one of the New Mexicans awarded an escudo de honor by the Mexican government. The report of the sheep he distributed is but a small part of the many documents that tell us how New Mexico responded to the Texas expedition. Among these is a brief, unintended glimpse of a wife's concern for the safety of a husband as well as the role he played in this brief shining moment in New Mexico history.

Taos Contributes for Support of the Troops, 1843

The year 1843 was stressful in New Mexico. As early as the spring of 1842, officials had been receiving reports from traders along the frontier and through diplomatic channels that the Texans were organizing a campaign to invade New Mexico to exact their revenge for the capture of the 1841 Texas–New Mexico expedition. By early 1843, it became clear that the Texans, desirous of the revenue New Mexico derived from the US merchant caravans, planned to attack and confiscate the next scheduled caravan as it passed through Texan territory, which they claimed included all the territory east of the Rio Grande.

The military disaster that New Mexico suffered at the hands of the Texans in late spring of 1843 is a story for another time. This column will concentrate on an example of the extraordinary, and often frustrating, efforts New Mexican officials and their military leaders went through to provide for the troops and militia that were gathered to counter the Texan threat and defend the frontier. New Mexico's Spanish- and Mexican-era archives make it clear that the presidio troops suffered greatly due to the persistent lack of resources to pay their salaries and, quite often, even provide for their rations, uniforms, and other basic needs. In order to equip and feed the presidio troops, militia, and auxiliary troops that were sent from Chihuahua to counter the

Texan threat, Governor Manuel Armijo and northern prefect Juan Andres Archuleta issued a desperate plea for funds, flour, meat, and other supplies. Our Mexican-era records have numerous examples of loans and contributions made by individuals in response to those pleas, but so far only one document has surfaced listing the individuals who responded to the appeals for assistance from a specific jurisdiction, and itemizes what they contributed.

In a document dated July 10, 1843, Pascual Martínez, justice of the peace for the Taos jurisdiction, and his cosignatory, Juan Ygnacio Martínez, submitted a list of the citizens who had pledged contributions to a "voluntary loan" that had been solicited for the "assistance and pay" of the troops. The list is headed by the Reverend Antonio José Martínez, who contributed one hundred twenty pesos in cash and one hundred eighty pesos in flour, rams, and other items for a total of 300 pesos. The remaining contributions are all listed by name with the honorific title of don:

Blas Trujillo: 25 pesos cash and 25 rams
Juan de Jesus Vigil: 100 rams (*carneros primales*)
Gregorio Lucero: 20 pesos cash and 10 rams
Juan Manuel Lucero: 12 rams
Ignacio Gonzales: a fat ox
Juan Domingo Tafoya: a fat cow
Pablo Suazo: a team (*yunta*) of oxen and one cow
Mateo Gomes: 25 rams
Buenaventura Valdes: 5 pesos cash (on August 15)
Luis Lee: 100 flasks of aguardiente [liquor, typically brandy]

Antonio Suares Montero: 15 pesos in flour
Pablo Trujillo: 100 pesos, an ox, and four fanegas of flour (in August)
José María Martines: 15 fanegas of wheat in August and the rest of what he has in August
Juan Felipe Romero: one fanega of flour
Lorenzo Cordova: one fat ox
José Ignacio Valdes: 20 fanegas of wheat in September
Maríano Martines: 5 fanegas of wheat in September
Juan Pacheco: 3 pesos
Matías Vigil: a horse
Gabriel Montaño: item not specified in August and one almud of flour now
Juan Antonio Martines: 4 pesos in flour and meat
José María Quintana: 6 rams
Juan Valdes: 6 fanegas of wheat
Juan Miguel Baca: 4 fanegas of wheat in September
Juvencio Naranjo: 2 pesos in unspecified hides (*cueros*)
José Gregorio Martines: 25 rams and 20 pesos cash
Francisco Xaramillo: 2 pesos cash
José de la Merced Romero: 2 pesos cash
José Manuel Sandoval: 4 fanegas of wheat in September
Manuel Romero: 3 fanegas of wheat in September
José Trujillo: one fanega of wheat in September
José Rafael Cordova del Rancho: one fanega of wheat in September
Abran Ledu: 6 fanegas of wheat in September
Bautista Yara: one fanega of corn now and 2 of wheat in September

Pablo Ribera: 5 pesos and 5 fanegas of flour in September
Teodoro Romero 2o [*segundo*]: 25 pesos and unspecified fanegas of flour
Cornelio Vigil: one ox and 25 pesos cash
José Quintana: 6 rams
Ricardo Vigil: 2 elaborated hides (*de marca*)
Juan Julian Martines: 2 fanegas of flour in September
Miguel Sanches: 2 sheep and 2 fanegas of flour, the latter in September
Juan Ygnacio Martines: 6 fanegas of wheat

In all, the contributions from Taos totaled slightly more than 1,000 pesos in value. Subsequent records do not reflect how much of this was actually collected considering that much of the flour pledged would not be available until the harvest in September. One can also wonder how much of the cash contributed made its way to the treasury in Santa Fe and how much of the liquor and livestock fed and comforted the troops. Regardless, this list does serve as an example of what the citizens of the Taos jurisdiction were willing and able to contribute toward support of the troops in times of crisis.

The 1844 Ute Raid on Santa Fe

The late summer of 1844 was a tense time in northern New Mexico. In August of that year, several capitancillos, chiefs of the Ute tribe, arrived at Abiquiú with many warriors and their families. The prefect of that region, Colonel Juan Andres

Archuleta, reported that the Utes were demanding the return of three Navajo captives they had obtained during an earlier campaign against that tribe. The captives had apparently been confiscated by Mexican officials, and they wanted them returned. The Utes also demanded compensation for ten of their warriors who had been killed in that war with the Navajos.

Local officials at Abiquiú attempted to pacify the Utes by agreeing to return the captives. The Utes left, according to Archuleta, "in friendly terms," but returned within a few hours, made their camp, and commenced a series of disturbances, the most serious of which was setting their horses free to roam in the surrounding cultivated fields, causing great damage to the ongoing harvest.

The Utes were finally convinced to go to Santa Fe and present their grievances directly to Governor Mariano Martínez. Forewarned by Archuleta's reports, Governor Martínez made arrangements to receive his impending guests and ordered some sheep slaughtered for meat, along with tobacco and other gifts to present to the Utes when they arrived at the capital.

Six Ute chiefs and one hundred eighty warriors arrived at Santa Fe on the afternoon of September 5. According to Governor Martínez's report, the Utes entered the city mounted on good horses and well armed, moving about in a manner that suggested they were prepared for, if not actually looking for a fight. At the governor's invitation, they agreed to dismount, make their camp, and eat.

The following morning of September 6, the Utes continued what the governor's report described as their "suspicious movements." They refused the breakfast they were offered and threw

Figure 18. Ute Braves of the Kah-poh-teh (Capote) band of northern New Mexico, 1874. Timothy O'Sullivan photo, Library of Congress.

the gifts they were given onto the street. Shortly afterward, the six chiefs sent word to the governor that they wanted to speak with him, and he agreed to do so, inviting them to join him in a room inside the Palace of the Governors. Through their interpreter, they informed Governor Martínez that they were dissatisfied with the gifts they had received, and Martínez ordered several other items brought to them.

The Utes apparently remained unhappy, and Panasiyave, one of their principal chiefs, began to express his opinion of the gifts in "very indecorous terms." Governor Martínez, who seems to have begun to lose his patience, suggested they leave for a while and allow him time to consider their complaints and to send for some of the gifts they had requested. The suggestion apparently infuriated the Utes, and Panasiyave stepped up to Martínez and began to hit or poke him in the chest with his fist. The governor pushed Panasiyave away and warned him to keep his distance. At this, several Utes drew their knives and Panasiyave lunged at Martínez, brandishing a hatchet. As Panasiyave lunged at him, the governor managed to grab a chair and strike his attacker, knocking him to the ground. Two of the governor's orderlies and other officers in attendance held the other five chiefs at bay, along with several other warriors who had poured into the room through a window.

A general melee followed, with soldiers and several citizens joining the fight. Within moments, eight Utes lay dead, and the remainder, realizing their chiefs had been killed, quickly made their escape to the country. A troop of fifty soldiers equipped with a cannon was hastily organized and sent in pursuit of the retreating Utes. A running fight, which lasted most of the day, ensued during which five more Utes were killed and three soldiers wounded, but the troops were unable to overtake the main body of Utes and most escaped into the hills.

Some accounts differ somewhat with the official reports found in our Mexican Archives of New Mexico from which this story is taken. One of the notable differences is from Demetrio Pérez's 1913 account of the incident in which he tells how the governor's "valiant wife, doña Teresita," entered the room just as her husband was being attacked and having "the presence of mind" to have his sword with her, handed it to him, "that he might defend himself." Martínez's report fails to mention that his wife was present or that he used a sword to defend himself.

Thus ended what the history books often call "The Ute Invasion of Santa Fe." However, as in reviewing the official records of this incident, one might wonder if instead of an invasion, this may have been an ambush orchestrated by government officials frustrated by the seemingly incessant raids by the many hostile tribes that populated the New Mexican frontier.

CHAPTER FOUR

The Judicial System in Mexican-Era New Mexico

A Complete Lack of Lawyers!

One of the persistent complaints of New Mexico's Spanish- and Mexican-era governors and other officials was the inability of local judicial officials to consult with and seek advice from for the handling and processing of judicial cases. During his first term as governor, Manuel Armijo pointed out this shortcoming to the territorial governing council, noting that New Mexico's educational system was incapable of producing literate and qualified alcaldes to whom the law assigned primary responsibility for administering an effective judicial system.

Armijo indicated that New Mexico had very few people capable of developing a competent judicial case and there was not a single lawyer in the territory with whom officials could consult, making it necessary to seek advice from Chihuahua or Durango, a process that delayed decisions, often for months. Even then, the few lawyers at these places were busy and preferred not to deal with poorly developed cases from New Mexico. Armijo indicated that a good educational system could eventually remedy this situation, but for now they needed an *Asesor* (assessor) and a district tribunal funded by the federal government that would function as a court of appeals to review and rule on issues of law and due process.

As 1828 was coming to a close, Armijo lamented to the Minister of Justice in Mexico of New Mexico's desperate need for trained men and judicial tribunals that local officials could consult. He indicated that New Mexico's alcaldes were generally ignorant of the law and insisted on following the Spanish-era practice of referring cases to the gefe politico as a court of appeals, a custom he had continued although he understood he should not be doing so. In June of 1829, Juan Estevan Pino developed a proposal for the governing council that recommended the formation of juzgados (courts), which was forwarded to Manuel de Jesús Rada, New Mexico's delegate to the national congress.

Rada apparently convinced congress to take much-needed action, and in a circular dated August 29, 1829, the Mexican president ordered the appointment of an Asesor for each territory with whom local judges could consult on civil and criminal cases. Within a month, *Licenciado* J. Eluterio María de la Garza had applied to the Ministry of Justice for the position and on October 17, 1829, was appointed as New Mexico's Asesor at a salary of 3,000 pesos a year. On December 8, Garza notified the diputación that he was preparing to leave the capital (Mexico City) within fifteen days and begin traveling to New Mexico.

But it was not to be. On January 22, 1830, Garza, writing from Chihuahua, reported issues with his health and indicated that he would proceed when feeling better but pointed out that New Mexico did not have funds to pay his salary so he could not proceed without financial assistance. A month later he was still in Chihuahua, asking if he could establish his residence there and requested an advance of fifty pesos in lieu of salary. By early May, Garza was still in Chihuahua complaining that his health was still "broken" and that the funds he had been advanced were not enough to continue the journey to New Mexico. That noted, he submitted his resignation in part because he had not been allowed to remain in Chihuahua and do the job from there. Officials from the Ministry of Justice quickly accepted his resignation and ordered that the 1,000 pesos they had advanced on his salary would have to be reimbursed. Over the next several months, Garza haggled with Mexican officials over the issue of his salary and lamented that he could not afford to reimburse the advance he had received. Responses from Treasury officials were not kind, adamantly insisting that prompt payment was required. It is not clear when or even if the issue was ever resolved.

New Mexico lost its Asesor before he ever arrived. However, in June 1830, almost as soon as Garza's resignation was accepted by judicial officials in Mexico, they appointed Licenciado Mariano Guerra Manzanares to the position. Manzanares' appointment did not last long either. Little more than a month later, he resigned the position, citing his health.

The position did not remain vacant for long. On September 23, 1830, Licenciado Antonio Barreiro was appointed Asesor for New Mexico and advanced six months' salary as a travel allowance. Barreiro accepted the position on September 26, 1830, and by late December he had arrived in Chihuahua. While there he received news from New Mexico of massive snowfalls that were making life miserable even for natives used to such a "cruel and strong climate" (tan crudo y fuerte clima). Barreiro indicated that he could not risk traveling under these conditions and would remain in Chihuahua until mid-February, or when travel conditions improved.

In early March 1831, a party of eight soldiers and one sergeant from the Santa Fe presidio were sent to meet Barreiro and relieve the escort that had accompanied him from San Elizario. Barreiro and his escort arrived in Santa Fe on March 29, 1831, took his oath of office on April 5, and according to a report from Governor José Antonio Chaves, resumed his duties that same day. The career of Antonio Barreiro will certainly provide material for future columns.

Murder During New Mexico's Mexican Period

New Mexico's Mexican-era archives reveal more than three dozen cases in which a suspicious death was reported or investigated by judicial authorities. At least a dozen of these seem to be clear-cut cases of murder and provide a fairly complete picture of the manner in which the Mexican judicial system functioned. However, this same documentation shows that very few of these cases were concluded by an official determination of guilt or innocence, and none of the few that were fully adjudicated show the final imposition of a sentence.

Four of these cases involve foreigners as the murder victim or suspects in a suspicious death and several other cases involve a husband murdering his wife. In the earliest of these, Manuel Gallegos of Santa Cruz de la Cañada was accused of strangling his wife in 1834. Investigation showed a bruise across her throat, and when Gallegos confessed to the crime, he noted that he had strangled her with a rawhide strap. When asked why he did it, he simply stated that she argued with him everywhere they went, and the impression one gets is of a hen-pecked husband who simply couldn't take it anymore.

The Gallegos case is well documented and shows a typical prosecution. After preliminary interrogations were done and testimony taken at the local level, the case continued with the formal appointment of a *promotor fiscal*, a prosecutor that handled the case for the government, and a *defensor* to represent the rights of the accused. The promotor in the Gallegos case urged punishment to the full extent of the law, which, if it was determined to have been premeditated murder, meant death. The defensor took a different tack. He had no choice other than to admit his client's guilt, especially since Gallegos had confessed. Instead, he argued that premeditation could not have been a factor due to ignorance. What else, he noted, could have explained Gallegos's failure to try and escape an uneventful capture? The crime, he argued, certainly deserved to be punished, but not with the death penalty.

Unable or unwilling to decide if there was premeditation and therefore a capital crime, a consultation was sought from someone more knowledgeable about the law. The final notation in the case indicates that the file was sent to the Licenciado Agustín Abellano in Chihuahua because there were no lawyers or other individuals in New Mexico qualified to review the case. The documentation ends at this point with no further indication of what happened to Gallegos.

Incomplete case files make it impossible to determine the ultimate outcome of the several wife murder cases in the Mexican-era archives, although the issue of guilt is seldom in doubt. For example, in the 1842 proceedings against Rafael Montoya for the stabbing death of his wife, María Alvina Gonzales's deathbed declaration implicated her husband, and Montoya later confessed to the crime, citing suspected infidelities. In 1846 the body of María Angelica Herrera was discovered near the Pueblo of Cochiti, her head crushed and a bloody stone found nearby. Her husband, Juan Antonio Chaves, was found at home, arrested, placed in irons, and turned over to the alcalde of the pueblo for safekeeping. When questioned, he confessed to the murder. He explained that his wife had been absent from their home for three days, so he went looking for her. When he found her gathering firewood near the pueblo, he ordered her home, but she refused. Instead, she struck him with her fist and threw a rock at him. Chaves then picked up the rock and struck her with it until she was dead, and went home.

The Chaves case is well developed and his defensor argued that while guilt could not be denied, the case should not be considered premeditated murder and therefore adjudicated as a capital crime. He instead described the crime as "incidental homicide without premeditation," in which the suspect may have had inadequate understanding of the law and had not understood the severity and consequence of homicide, especially in a society where the woman was expected to be obedient to her husband.

Unfortunately, there are no documented conclusions to any of the murder cases in the Mexican Archives of New Mexico, so we cannot determine what punishments were handed out

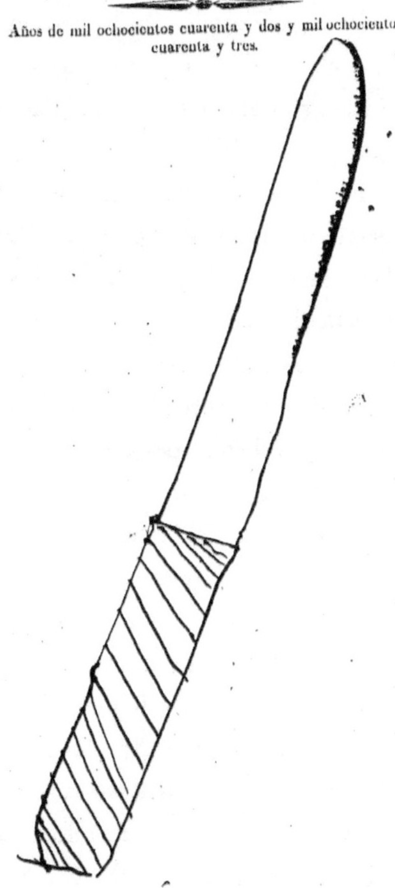

Figure 19. Outline of murder weapon, "Proceedings against Rafael Montoya," MANM: 1842 Judicial Proceedings, Rio Abajo Jurisdiction.

for murder by the Mexican judicial system in New Mexico. It is clear, however, that officials given the responsibility of conducting these investigations and trials were extremely careful in their deliberations. When it came to serious crimes such as murder, these judges made every effort to see that the suspects were afforded due process and justice. Readers interested in learning more about this subject, I encourage you to read *Murder and Justice in Frontier New Mexico, 1821–1846* (University of New Mexico Press, 1997) by Jill Mocho. It is the only comprehensive and well-researched publication available on the topic.

Foreigner's Views of New Mexico's Judicial System

It has been noted many times in these pages that the Mexican Archives of New Mexico is an overlooked and unappreciated documentary treasure. Much of what has been written about our Mexican era is based on the dozens of books and memoirs by and about the Americans who traveled to New Mexico over the Santa Fe Trail. Over the years, I have published excerpts from some of these and commented on the erroneous and quite often racist commentary that was left behind by these authors. One can often wonder whether events related by these authors actually took place or unfolded in the manner described, prompting one to look for evidence of what they wrote in our Mexican-era archives.

One of the most widely read and quoted books of this genre is Josiah Gregg's *The Commerce of the Prairies*. Originally published in 1844, it is a valuable source of information regarding trade and commerce over the Santa Fe Trail. In one of his later chapters, Gregg writes briefly about the murder of a young American he called "Daley" at the gold fields of Real del Oro, south of Santa Fe, during the winter of 1837–1838. Gregg is highly critical of the Mexican judicial system that he assumed allowed the suspects to go unpunished, and of Governor Manuel Armijo's presumed failure to act until he was forced to do so by pressure from the Americans.

To Gregg's credit, the case actually exists in the Mexican Archives of New Mexico. "Daley" was actually Andres (Andrew) Doyle, who was killed at Real del Oro on February 28, 1838, during a robbery of John Langham's store, where Doyle worked as the cashier. The extensive, although incomplete case file shows that what Gregg describes as indifference and disregard for the law was a well-documented concern for due process, although there was one significant delay in the case due to the all-too-common escape of the suspects from jail.

The records show that little more than a week after the robbery and murder, four suspects were arrested in the vicinity of the pueblos of San Yldefonso and San Juan de los Caballeros. Two of the men, Salvador Barela y Borrego and Diego Martín, confessed to the crime. A review of their interrogation seems to show premeditation, making this a capital crime punishable by death, if convicted. When the investigation and reports were turned over to Governor Armijo, he forwarded the case to Chihuahua for legal review before referring it to the Supreme Court for confirmation of the sentence. While this was being done, Barela y Borrego and Martín escaped from the jail at Real del Oro and remained on the loose until they were rearrested at San Juan the following July of 1839. While the record does not provide details of the escape or show why the escapees were able to remain free for so long, it does appear that officials were prodded to act by pressure and complaints from American merchants.

Josiah Gregg left New Mexico in 1840. By then, the suspects had been recaptured, the confessions reaffirmed, and Barela y Borrego and Martín sentenced to death. Their death sentence specified that the executions were to be carried out in front of the place where their "nefarious crime" had been committed. However, final approval of the sentence had to be reviewed by legal counsel in Chihuahua and, as was typical of the time, responses were long in coming. For nearly three years, the case was sent back and forth until finally, legal advisors concluded that the case had been bungled and tasked local judicial officials to resubmit the case more in line with what they considered due process. However, the case file ends in 1843 without conclusion, and with the fate of the convicts pending. There is no indication that the case was prosecuted any further or that the sentences of death were carried out.

Gregg was correct that the suspects were freed, although they were not, as he charged, allowed to "run at large." They were released on bond, as provided by law, and their appearance at final sentence was guaranteed by a competent person. Gregg clearly misinterpreted the delays in achieving "justice," presuming that the Mexican judicial system should have functioned like American courts, where a capital murder trial and conviction could be obtained in a single day and a death sentence carried out within a month.

This is but one example of how we often assume that those who wrote about events of long ago had to have been right because they were presumably eyewitnesses to the events. These presumptions on our part have led to the creation of myths and misperceptions that have a broad exposure and influence that extends to the present. It's not that men such as Gregg were always wrong, it's just that we should take some time to fact-check before we presume they were right.

Jails in the Mexican Period (1821–1846)

Toward the end of the Spanish period, documentation begins to provide a fair, but still incomplete, idea of conditions in New Mexico jails. In 1820, Manuel Armijo, who would in a few years be appointed governor, was being held in jail at Santa Fe on charges of assaulting a priest in Albuquerque. His appeal of incarceration noted the appalling condition of the room where he was being held. He indicated that it was cold (the letter was written in January), and apparently windowless, because it was dark as night when the door was closed.

The same year of 1820, a bando, or decree, sent from Chihuahua ordered the improvement of jails and treatment of prisoners. The reforms prohibited the use of chains or irons except under specific orders of a judicial officer and specified that cells should have natural light for prisoners. It also ordered the destruction of instruments of torture, which may explain why we have no surviving examples of *grillos* (shackles), the *cepo* (stocks), or especially, the *bartolina,* which brings to mind an image of "the box" used in the motion picture *Cool Hand Luke.*

Under Mexican administration, some differences in terminology also appear, such as the use of *cárcel nacional* (national jail), instead of *cárcel pública* (public jail) to identify the jails in the territory. This period also seems to introduce the term calabozo, from which the English "calaboose" seems to derive. In 1823, the calabozo was located in the quartel, or military complex, of the presidio in Santa Fe.

An 1822 census that includes a list of jails in New Mexico shows that the villas of Santa Fe and Albuquerque had a formal jail. Whatever they were called, and despite efforts at reform, conditions apparently remained poor. An 1826 petition submitted on behalf of six men from Albuquerque being held in jail at Santa Fe described deplorable conditions that caused them "insufferable and immeasurable calamities." The petition asked the governor to release them on bond so they could find relief from the conditions under which they were being held, tend their fields, and see to the needs of their families.

These conditions are reflected in Antonio Barreiro's 1832 *Ojeada Sobre Nuevo-Mexico,* in which he described New Mexico's jails as "no other than certain filthy rooms" that were scarcely dignified to be called jails. Curiously, Barreiro did not feel the prisoners held under these conditions were in dire straits. Instead, he noted critically, "they pass the time much diverted in merry frolics and chatter; and they take their imprisonment with the greatest ease, for at night they escape to dances (bailes) and by day to other diversions."

An 1838 letter tells us that Santa Fe's jail consisted of a few unhealthy and inhospitable rooms that were in poor repair. The letter noted that the jail was "a bed of fleas, louses, bed bugs, mice and other sickening and filthy insects, which . . . destroys the most robust health and brings the most remote illness to the human body."

All of this indicates that New Mexico's jails were very unpleasant and certainly unhealthy places, and consequently prisoners did all they could to keep their stay in them as short as possible. The Spanish and Mexican governments devoted few resources to this type of building, due in part to the fact that these judicial systems seldom used long prison sentences as a form of punishment. Instead, they utilized fines, terms at public labor, and restitution as sentences, and viewed imprisonment as a waste of money and resources.

Toward the end of the Mexican period, government officials were doing their best to make sure that local jurisdictions had adequate jails in which prisoners could be securely held. In late 1844, Governor Mariano Martínez ordered his prefects to have secure jails built in towns that did not have them. Scattered reports from various alcaldías for the period, including the Pueblo of Sandia and the plaza of Tomé, indicate that they had "secure jails" but do not provide descriptions of what these consisted or where they were located. There is also some indication that some of the "principal jails" in New Mexico (the report did not specify which ones) were attempting to establish *talleres de artes*, or work programs for their inmates.

This period also seems to have developed separate facilities for military and civilian prisoners. An 1845 case mentions that there was a public jail in Santa Fe where *presos paisanos* (civilian prisoners) were held. By early 1846, we also see municipal ordinances regulating the management of local jails and reports of the ayuntamiento of Santa Fe that list expenses for food for prisoners and the salary of a jailer. The same reports, however, also show expenses for making or repairing grillos, the same shackles that show up prominently in the early history of crime and punishment in New Mexico and continue well into the subsequent territorial and statehood periods.

Felipe Salas—*El Condenado a Muerte*?

During New Mexico's territorial period (1846–1912), several fascinating corridos (folk ballads) were written by or about individuals awaiting execution after being sentenced to death by a court of law. This author recently published an article in *La Crónica de Nuevo México*, the Historical Society of New Mexico journal, on five individuals, including one woman, whose sad and tragic stories were told by such ballads.

The oldest reference I have found to a ballad of this genre is entitled *El condenado a muerte* (The condemned to death), published by Arthur Leon Campa in *Spanish Folk—Poetry in New Mexico*. Campa says the author of the poem is unknown, but attributes the text to Rafael Lucero of El Pino, New Mexico. This corrido tells the story of an unnamed individual who was condemned to die on Wednesday, July 20, 1832. However, my own research and that of Jill Mocho in her book *Murder and Justice in Frontier New Mexico, 1821–1846* has found no evidence in New Mexico's Mexican-period civil and judicial records or church burial records of any executions by judicial fiat in New Mexico for that period. I have consequently concluded that the ballad is about an execution that took place in Mexico and was later published in one of the territory's Spanish-language newspapers.

Despite the lack of primary evidence for an execution by judicial fiat for that period, one case has intrigued me enough to consider that it may have been the story behind the unnamed individual in *El condenado a muerte*. A series of 1834 documents in the Mexican Archives of New Mexico (two years after the 1832 date in the corrido) concern the fate of Felipe Salas. Salas shows up in the historical record in a letter from the Mexican Supreme Court dated October 11, 1834. The letter, addressed to Santa Fe alcalde Juan Gallegos, the presiding judge in Salas's case, authorizes a death sentence for Felipe Salas but does not mention Salas's crime. The court also demanded that Gallegos confirm the method of execution when the sentence was carried out. There is no indication when the letter from the Supreme Court arrived in Santa Fe, but that December a dispute broke out between civilian and military authorities when Gallegos informed Blas de Hinojos, the comandante principal of the presidio garrison, that the execution was scheduled for December 5, 1834, and asked Hinojos to provide an escort of eight men to help carry it out. Hinojos responded that he could not assist with any arrangements for the execution beyond those of "security and custody" of the prisoner. He pointed out that the Salas execution was a civil matter and emphasized that the military was prohibited by law to assist in the execution of the prisoner, which was to be carried out by decapitation.

Local officials were probably squeamish about carrying out what would have certainly been a gruesome task and seemed unable to find any civilians willing to participate in the execution. Regardless, the issue remained unsettled for a year while local officials sought legal consultation from authorities in Mexico. Finally, on November 25, 1835, officials in Mexico confirmed Hinojos's contention that troops were prohibited from administering the death penalty in civil cases. The court also ruled that local officials needed to be prepared for such occasions by acquiring a *mascada*—an iron ring that was placed around the neck and used to garrote and break the neck of a condemned prisoner. They were also required to have an executioner (*verdugo*) available along with a squad of five to ten men paid from public funds to provide security for condemned prisoners. Felipe Salas's fate remains unknown as no record of an execution has come to light in our Mexican-era archives or the burial records of the Archdiocese of Santa Fe.

The corrido of our unnamed condenado a muerte tells of an impending death, the broken hearts of family, and contrary to what may have taken place in the Felipe Salas case, a military escort:

Miércoles viente de Julio	Wednesday, the twentieth of July
De ochocientos trienta y dos;	Of eighteen hundred thirty two;
Me llevan para el sepucro	They take me to the sepulcher
Para darle cuenta a Dios.	To make my accounting to God.
Me llevan pa' la capilla	They take me to the chapel

Bajando por escalones	Descending the steps
Quebrando los corazones	Breaking the hearts
Se los padres de familia.	Of parents of families.
Un sacerdote me auxilia,	A priest supports me,
Tropa me va acompañando,	Troops accompany me,
Las cornetas van tocando.	The trumpets are playing.
Ya sin remedio ninguno,	Now with no remedy,
Me llevan para el sepulcro	I am taken to my tomb
miercoles veinte de julio.	Wednesday, the twentieth of July.
En fin yo voy a llegar	At the end I will arrive
A donde voy a murir,	Where I am to die,
Me tengo que despedir	I must take my leave
Con mi voz muy lastimosa.	With my voice very saddened.

CHAPTER FIVE

Commerce and Trade

A Chance Meeting on the Eastern Plains

Prior to Mexican independence, New Mexico's economy consisted of five major elements—agriculture, livestock, bison, trade with Mexico, and trade with Native American tribes. The land, distributed to its citizens by a system of grants, produced crops, grazing for livestock, timber for firewood and building, and game for hunting. Flocks of sheep, goats, and herds of oxen and cattle provided milk, meat for the table, hides for tanning, and wool that was spun and woven into cloth and blankets for personal use and trade. Thousands of rams and locally produced goods were exported to northern Mexico every year and sold for cash or traded for goods. Many communities had ciboleros, men who traveled to the eastern plains every fall to hunt bison. Wagons loaded with jerked and dried bison meat, and thousands of bison hides that were tanned and traded, helped many communities survive what were often severe and lean winters.

The elements of commerce and trade during the Spanish era are fully reflected in Governor Fernando Chacón's 1803 report on New Mexico's economy and natural resources. Chacón's report provides us with a fascinating overview of agriculture, industry, arts, commerce, and economic conditions in the New Mexico of two centuries ago. Chacón emphasized the importance of trade with the region's nomadic tribes along the northern frontier. At official trading opportunities called *rescates*, as well as frequent unofficial, illegal occasions, New Mexicans traded leather goods, hatchets, knives, scissors, piloncillo (lumps of sugar), corn and corn flour, bread, dried fruit, and punche, the native tobacco, in exchange for moccasins, wild colts, all types of pelts, bison meat, and human captives.

A significant change to New Mexico's commerce occurred in a chance encounter in the vicinity of present-day Las Vegas in the fall of 1821. By late 1821, Mexico had gained its independence from Spain, and indications are, New Mexico was well informed of the monumental events that were bringing impending change to its government. One issue, however, had not changed—frontier tribes continued to raid and harass New Mexico's pueblos and communities.

It was in the midst of these circumstances that militia captain Pedro Ignacio Gallego was ordered by Governor Facundo Melgares to organize an expedition to scout the frontier for trails of recent raiders. Gallego began his scout from Abiquiú on November 2, 1821, with 148 militia—a number that was augmented periodically along his route—and made his way to the Pueblo of Jémez where he received orders from Governor Melgares directing him to head east. Gallego's expedition made its way east through Santo Domingo, Galisteo, and to the "Poblacion del Vado," where he halted and took inventory of his force, which had grown to 445 men, 123 armed with firearms and the rest with bows and arrows. He also noted that they had 356 pack animals. This was, by any standard of the time, a significant undertaking.

Gallego and his forces departed Vado on November 12. The following day, in his own understated words, "about 3:30 P.M. encountered six Americans at the Puertocito of la Piedra Lumbre. They parleyed with me. . . . Not understanding their words nor any of the signs they made, I decided to return to Vado. Nothing further occurred." With these few words and no further comment, Gallego escorted the Americans to Vado, where either along the way, or at Vado itself, Vicente Villanueva "presented himself" to serve as interpreter. Gallego left the Americans with Villanueva so he could escort them to Santa Fe and resumed his expedition.

On November 13, 1821, New Mexico's history was changed forever. On that day, Gallego encountered the trading expedition of William Becknell, who is often credited with being the first American to initiate legal commerce between New Mexico and the United States along what became known as the Santa Fe Trail. Becknell's journal, which has been widely published and its contents debated, notes, with an apparent sigh of relief, that "On Tuesday the 13th, we had the satisfaction of meeting with a party of Spanish troops. Although the difference of our language would not admit of conversation . . . their reception of us, fully convinced us of their hospitable disposition and friendly feelings."

Becknell and his party arrived in Santa Fe on November 17, 1821, and met with Governor Facundo Melgares the following day. His journal notes that he was cordially received by the governor, who apparently made it clear that further commercial trade with the Americans would be welcomed. During his short stay in New Mexico, Becknell and his companions managed to dispose of the goods he had to trade and by most accounts returned home with a substantial profit. His success may be reflected by the possibly apocryphal tale of Becknell's arrival back in Franklin, Missouri, where it is said they tore open their rawhide packs, noisily spilling silver pesos on the stone pavement. No doubt such a stunt would have prompted countless adventurers and men of enterprise to direct their sights westward to the settlements of New Mexico, adding another element, for better or worse, to New Mexico's economy.

Regulation of Trade

History books tell us that the Santa Fe Trail opened in 1821, the same year Mexico gained its independence from Spain. The general impression one often gets is that following that fateful meeting between Captain Pedro Ignacio Gallego and William Becknell in November 1821, the borders between New Mexico and the United States magically opened, ushering in an era of the free flow of people and trade between the two countries.

The reality was that, as with all foreign countries, whatever commerce took place between New Mexico and the United States was regulated and closely watched by officials of the Mexican government in Santa Fe. The records of the Mexican Archives of New Mexico make it clear that by 1823, officials in Santa Fe were concerned that Americans were importing goods without

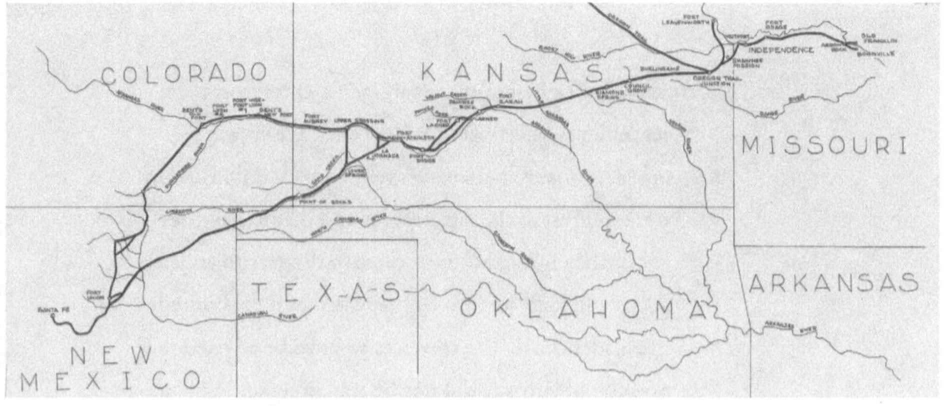

Figure 20. Santa Fe Trail. Courtesy of the Santa Fe Trail Association.

paying the required tariffs. Officials were especially concerned that these men were hunting beaver illegally, to the detriment of local residents. Beaver trapping was a branch of industry reserved by law exclusively to Mexican citizens.

One of the earliest efforts by officials in Santa Fe to assist customs officers along the border to cope with the influx of *estranjeros* (foreigners), were the instructions issued by administrator Juan Bautista Vigil in early April 1825. The instructions were issued to Severino Martín and Rafael Luna, the customs officers at New Mexico's northern frontier in Taos. These consist of seven sections as follows:

1. Upon receiving notice that foreigners were approaching the borders, they were to request assistance from the local chief of militia and proceed to the frontier and determine if these foreigners proposed to introduce commercial goods into New Mexico.

2. At some point before these foreigners entered any settlements, they were to show their passports to prove they were persons traveling in good faith. They were to present their passports and invoices of the goods they wished to introduce to the territory. The packs and load were to be inspected and prohibited items identified. The travelers were to be advised that prohibited items could not be traded or sold unless they obtained an exemption from the governor or principal customs officer in Santa Fe.
3. If their passports were not in order, the cargo was to be closely examined and compared to the published tariff listings. The goods were to be impounded and sent to Santa Fe for review by the administrator (Vigil) and the proper tariffs applied.
4. If any of the foreigners demanded the personal presence of the administrator in the field, they were to do so formally, in writing and under the obligation that they were to pay for the expenses of the trip. The written request was to be sent to Santa Fe by the local customs officers along with any invoices, passports, and other related documents.
5. When contraband was discovered or an estranjero (or local accomplice) attempted to defraud the government, the nearest judicial official was to formally open a case, take charge of the disputed goods, and place the suspects under bond to assure their appearance in court. If found guilty, the person's goods were to be confiscated and subject to sale at public auction.

6. Until all these steps were taken, proper *guias* (passports) issued, and approval obtained from the administrator, no goods could be sold or traded. Violation of this regulation could result in the loss of all the merchant's goods.
7. If local officials had any doubts on how to proceed or deal with a situation, they were to suspend all activities until the administrator was consulted.

Records show that similar regulations were observed through much of the Mexican period. Escorts of militia or presidio troops from Santa Fe were regularly sent to meet approaching commercial caravans once they had crossed into Mexican territory at the Napeste (Arkansas River), Mexico's northern border. The idea was to meet the caravan before anyone had a chance to disperse or merchants had the opportunity to hide goods in order to avoid paying tariffs. Every load was supposed to be inspected, and suspected contraband confiscated. In 1831 all the stores in Santa Fe were ordered closed while officials went through each one after they had received word that some contraband goods had gotten through.

The tariffs collected every year were important to New Mexico. The revenue generated from the American merchants constituted the principal source of income for government operations during much of the Mexican period. Meticulously maintained records show that funds collected were immediately paid out to cover the often-overdue salaries of government officials, troops, and even loans that had been made to the government with the projected income as collateral.

CHAPTER FIVE

Antonio Armijo and the Old Spanish Trail

It has been said that the Old Spanish Trail is neither "old" nor "Spanish." The Trail, which has been designated a National Historic Trail by the National Park Service, is a series of trails New Mexicans used to trade with the Utes and other tribes in the region that we now know as southwest Colorado and Utah, and which eventually ended up being routes that connected New Mexico to California.

An overland route connecting New Mexico to the new missions being established in California had long been sought by Spanish officials and traders. As early as the mid-eighteenth century, attempts were made to establish such a route, the best known being the expedition of the Franciscan friars Domínguez and Escalante in 1776. The friars failed in their efforts to reach California, but it is clear from their published reports that much of the region they traversed was well known to New Mexicans.

The earliest well-documented description of a route from New Mexico to California was pioneered by Antonio Armijo in 1829. The journal of Armijo's pioneering journey was submitted by Governor José Antonio Chaves to officials in Mexico on May 14, 1830. What we know about the Armijo expedition is based mainly on Governor Chaves's letter of transmittal, which was published in the *Registro Oficial*, a publication of the Mexican government. The paper broke the news of Armijo's expedition in the June 5, 1830, issue of the *Registro* under the headline, "Road discovered from the Pueblo of Abiquiú in the territory of New Mexico to Alta California" and then published the journal itself in the June 18 issue.

Governor Chaves's letter tells us that Armijo left the community of Abiquiú with either thirty or sixty (the print is unclear) men who took along a supply of goods manufactured in New Mexico to trade with the Californians. With a couple of exceptions, Armijo's journal does not mention much about the men who accompanied him or specify the goods they took, but these were likely blankets and other wool products, bison skins, and tanned hides that could be loaded and transported on pack animals.

The printed version of Antonio Armijo's journal tells us he left the jurisdiction of Abiquiú on November 7, 1829, on his way to discovery of the "road to the Californias." According to the Chaves letter Armijo did so "without a map, compass, or any other guide." The expedition made its way west to the Rio Puerco that first day, took a day of rest on the eighth, and then proceeded west, noting the destination they reached with each day's travel. The places Armijo names have been the subject of numerous articles and debates by researchers attempting to trace the exact route they took. Some place-names he mentions are well known, such as their arrival at the Navajo River two weeks into the journey, where they encountered a Navajo ranchería and paid the Navajos eleven mares to guide and safely escort the expedition through Navajo territory.

As they continued west, they encountered a settlement of Payuches without incident, noting that the members of this tribe were peaceful (*mansos*). Several days later they encountered another settlement of Native Americans, which they did not name, but noted that they wore earrings on their noses. By late January 1830, it seems clear that they were running short of supplies and found it necessary to eat a horse and a mule, noting specifically that the mule they ate belonged to Miguel Valdes.

Fortunately for the expedition, they were finally approaching their destination. On January 27, the day after they butchered Miguel Valdes's mule, they encountered members of their expedition who had been out in search of Rafael Rivera, who had gone missing. These scouts (*cortada*) had apparently reached the "rancho de San Bernadino" and acquired supplies and other relief (*bastimento*). Newly supplied and no doubt relieved, the expedition proceeded until they reached the mission of San Gabriel Arcangel on January 31.

Antonio Armijo's journal says almost nothing about their stay at the mission or what they did during the entire month of February 1830. They did manage to sell their goods and purchased mules, horses, and other livestock. Indications are, several of the group decided to go to Sonora while the rest began the journey back to New Mexico on March 1. Armijo's journal ends with the notation that he arrived at the Pueblo of Jémez on April 25, 1830. Despite its brevity and lack of details, Antonio Armijo's day-by-day description of the route is considered one of the most complete of all the diaries that provide details of the route that developed between New Mexico and California, and which opened trade between provinces along what became known as the Old Spanish Trail.

An *Estranjero's* Proposal, 1832

One of the fascinating elements of New Mexico's Mexican period regards the activities of estranjeros, the foreigners who traveled to New Mexico to trade, often took up permanent residence, and became prominent in local and territorial affairs. Local officials were often puzzled by their aggressive nature and behavior, and had to develop laws and practices to deal with these foreigners' demands and expectations.

One such situation developed in 1832 when George Pratt, a US citizen residing in Santa Fe, submitted a proposal to the territorial diputación seeking a thirty-year concession of land sufficient to establish a saw mill (*un molino de rajar tablason*) and a tannery near Santa Fe at the site known as *Corral Viejo* (old corral). If he was granted the concession, Pratt proposed to return the land and any improvements at the end of thirty years.

The diputación considered Pratt's proposal at its July 16, 1832, session. It seems, however, that the request prompted the legislative body to discuss the fact that a number of foreigners were already illegally utilizing the water, timber, and other resources in the mountains around Santa Fe. A proposal developed by Juan Rafael Ortiz concluded that the activities of these foreigners were detrimental to the common use of the community's ejidos (common lands) and that they should be forced to shut down or at least charged a fee for such use.

A committee consisting of Antonio Sandoval, Padre Antonio José Martínez, and Julian Tenorio submitted the following recommendations to the diputación on July 18, 1832:

Most Excellent Sir:

The commission charged by your Excellency regarding the exposition of Mr. [Juan Rafael] Ortiz for the imposition of fees (or taxes) on the manufacture of aguardiente (whiskey or hard liquor often translated as brandy) and lumber mills returns the following reflections:

It is clear and evident that in the practice (or exercise) of the said manufactures of aguardiente, the foreigners who have these, consume community (or common) resources to a greater extent than citizens utilize for their use. For example, a house that consumes wood, at the most, suffices with three or four carts each month. A still that manufactures aguardiente consumes 12–15. Considering the benefits of what they produce from a fanega of grain that gives 32–40 *quartillos* of aguardiente, and this computes, if sold at 3 reales, to 12–15 pesos per fanega, which at the time of harvest, costs them 1 or 2 pesos at most, and this paid in products at twice the price they are traded. They then collect this money (cash) for their aguardiente, which hinders further business (or trade) that our citizens could have with this resource.

As well, the lumber mills can be looked at in almost the same terms because in certain ways these prejudice the citizens that have this occupation for their livelihood [note: this is a double meaning; this competes with citizens who produce lumber and reduces availability of trees for wood cutters]. Finally, it must be considered, that even if the stated advantages were not so in the two types of industry noted, some fee should be imposed because they are foreigners that benefit from our resources, such as is regularly done by law in the states of our Republic.

As such, the commission recommends that such duties (taxes) should be extended to all the manufacture of aguardiente and lumber mills in all the territory under the following articles, subject to the deliberation of your Excellence:

1. That each manufacturer of aguardiente pay 3 pesos per month;
2. That foreigners that cut lumber (split boards) pay 2 pesos per month for each saw they operate;
3. That the collection and accounting of these fees be assigned to a person of confidence chosen by the respective ayuntamiento, to whom will be granted ten percent of what he collects in the district where such establishments exist;
4. What is collected from these in the capital pertain to the *fondo de veneficencia* (benevolent fund) and what is collected in Taos, where there are such establishments, and in other districts where they may be placed, it is destined for the municipal funds of the same;
5. That the charges be effective from now provisionally while it is passed in due form to the Supreme Government for approval or denial;
6. That this said exposition and the recommendation of this commission be submitted to the Supreme Government for the purposes of the previous article;
7. And lastly, a copy of the above be forwarded by his Excellency's secretary to the gefe politico so he can carry them out as per article five.

I have not found whether these recommendations were approved or whether Pratt's proposal was accepted at this time. However, by 1836 Santa Fe's ayuntamiento had implemented license fees for foreigners who wanted to cut timber around the city. It seems clear that New Mexicans were beginning to realize that the activities of foreigners were impacting the environment and threatening their economic livelihood and that they needed to do something about it. It may already have been too late.

The Richest Men in New Mexico

One often reads about individuals who were described as rich at various points in the history of New Mexico. Family histories often include stories about an ancestor who was considered rich or well to do until some misfortune befell the family. There are various types of documentation that can show us which individuals or families were in fact rich. Wills, for example, are a common source of such information. Wills usually list all the material goods left behind by a person and provide valuable information about their relative wealth.

However, other sources of such information show up in the archives that often allow us to gauge not only wealth, but influence. The most interesting of these are the various assessments made by the government to individuals in response for requests made by Spain or the Mexican government for donations, or *donativos*. These collections were meant to meet specific financial emergencies and included a category of "forced loans" imposed by both central and local governments. There are many examples of these. In early 1845, for example, New Mexico's Department Assembly decreed a loan of 12,000 pesos to meet the expenses of defending the frontier against the various tribes as well as the reported threats from Texas. The decree assessed the 12,000 pesos among what it described as the "leading capitalists," or businessmen, of New Mexico.

The first, or central district, that consisted of Santa Fe and its surrounding settlements, was assessed 1,700 pesos as follows:

José Montoya: 400 pesos
Juan Escolen (John Scolly): 600 pesos
Santiago Ulibarri: 300 pesos
Antonio Ortiz: 200 pesos
Vicente Ribera: 200 pesos

The second, or northern district, was assessed 1,900 pesos (please note that due to an apparent error in the math or because one or more individuals were left off the list, the amounts listed do not total the entire assessment):

José Jaramillo: 300 pesos
Pedro Martín: 500 pesos
Blas Trujillo: 500 pesos
Juan Vigil: 130 pesos
Gregorio Lucero: 200 pesos

The remainder of the loan, a total of 8,400 pesos, was assessed to the third, southern district:

Manuel Armijo, Pedro José Perea, Vicente Otero, Antonio Sandoval, and Antonio José and Juan Otero: 1,000 pesos each

Mariano Chaves, Juan Perea, Leandro Perea, Juan Cristobal Armijo, and Mariano Elisarri: 500 pesos each

José María Gutierrez: 400 pesos

Juan Armijo y Mestas: 300 pesos

Juan Gutierres: 200 pesos

This particular list points out not only the individuals who were considered to have the resources to contribute to the forced loan, but also demonstrates the relative discrepancy between the wealth in northern and southern New Mexico.

Thirty years earlier, in a response to an 1815 donativo requested by the Spanish government to help finance its various war expenses, Governor Alberto Maynes listed the individuals from the various settlements whom he felt most capable of making the largest contributions:

From Taos: Avan Cordova (200 pesos) and Pedro Martín (150 pesos)

Abiquiú: José Vigil (100 pesos)

Santa Cruz de la Cañada: Antonio Gallegos (200 pesos)

Santa Fe: Antonio Ortiz (300 pesos) and eight others at 100 pesos each

Albuquerque: Francisco Chaves (1000 pesos), Antonio Sandoval (300 pesos), and Joaquín Castillo (200 pesos)

Again, the rio abajo assessments reflect the apparent concentration of wealth in that region of the territory.

Another collection that demonstrates the relative wealth of individuals in the various regions in New Mexico comes from an 1819 report of the sheep and cattle donated by citizens to support the troops stationed in New Mexico. Bartolomé Baca and his wife contributed more than half of the 389 sheep collected from the rio abajo jurisdiction of Belen. That same year, a separate document shows Baca, who lived at the sitio of San Fernando, near Tomé, with assets that included 8,000 sheep, 214 cattle, 80 horses, and 25 tame mules. One can easily see how Bartolomé Baca would have easily qualified for inclusion on any list of the wealthiest people in New Mexico at that point in our history.

Diego Ramos's Journey to Mexico, 1840–1841

Readers of the monthly "Voices From the Past" columns are familiar with the author's tendency to get distracted by documents that mention someone or something unrelated to the current research topic. Such was the case while pouring over the bound copies of documents from Mexico's Archivo General de la Nación (AGN) in the France V. Scholes collection at the University of New Mexico.

In all the years I have researched New Mexico's Spanish and Mexican archives, I have never seen a document that can be described as a journal of someone who recorded their experiences when traveling along the camino real. This may be why my attention was drawn to a passport issued on October 21, 1840, by Governor Manuel Armijo that authorized Diego Ramos and three unnamed companions, all described as natives of the Pueblo of Sandia, to travel to Mexico City, capital of the republic, on unspecified "personal business." The proposed trip was obviously of some importance to them personally or to the pueblo because the passport includes a statement that describes Ramos and his companions as "peaceful citizens" and asks authorities along the way to treat them well and provide them with whatever assistance possible.

The document consists of three pages, with a series of certifications inserted by local officials at each place Ramos and his companions stopped to "check in." The date of this passport coincides with the traditional fall period when caravans departed New Mexico for Chihuahua and other places in Mexico but there is no indication that Ramos, his unidentified three companions, or several others that joined them along the route, made this trip as part of a scheduled caravan. The impression is that they made the trip on their own. Nevertheless, while this document is not a diary as such, it is the closest I have found to an itinerary of a trip from New Mexico to Mexico City along the camino real for that period.

The entries open with them checking in at Chihuahua on December 3, 1840, a month and a half after the passport was issued, then continue as follows:

> December 22, 1840, at Cerro Gordo, where the entry notes that although the passport was for Ramos and three others,

they arrived with four additional men, for a total of eight. Indications are, local officials issued another passport to include the additional parties.

January 5, 1841, at Rio Grande, where all was noted in order and that they moved on;

January 7, 1841, at Voquilla de [illegible];

January 10, 1841, at Paraje del Collote [Coyote] de la Hacienda del Rancho, where they were issued one head of livestock, presumably a sheep for food;

January 12, at San Antonio, where Ramos and five companions (they had apparently lost two since leaving Cerro Gordo) were given corn, meat, and three reales;

January 13, at Puesto del Coyote, they were provided pasture for their livestock and one real (1/8 of a peso) in coin;

January 14, at Refugio they were provided "succor" valued at four reales;

January 16, at Saucillos, they received some meat and two reales in cash;

January 17, at Aguas Calientes;

January 19, at [San Juan de los] Lagos;

> January 22, at Leon;
>
> January 23, at Silao, where they received one peso;
>
> January 25, Prefectura de Celody (?);
>
> January 26, at [illegible];
>
> January [illegible] at Cauchete (?);
>
> January 27, at Queretaro, where Ramos and five others were noted in the party;
>
> January 28, Prefectura de Arian (?);
>
> February 1, at Tepeqido del Rio (possibly Tepeji del Rio);
>
> February 2, at the Comandante Militar de Cautitlan (Cuautitlán?), where Ramos and two companions were provided with one peso and noted that they "continued their journey to Mexico."
>
> February 3, 1841, at the sub-prefecture of Habeposeth (?), where Ramos and three companions were noted continuing "towards this city."

This document allows us to trace some of the route Ramos and his companions took from New Mexico to Mexico City, but it is a bad copy, with several undecipherable place names and most not found in modern maps of Mexico. However, present-day locations, such as Cerro Gordo, San Juan de los Lagos, Leon, Queretaro, and others, are still along the ancient road and are described by Hal Jackson in *Following the Royal Road: A Guide to the Historic Camino Real de Tierra Adentro.*

The entries in Ramos's itinerary end as they are approaching Mexico City, and one can wonder about the purpose of their journey. This later question may have been answered in the recent book *Four Square Leagues: Pueblo Indian Land in New Mexico* by Malcolm Ebright, Rick Hendricks, and Richard W. Hughes. On page 131, they mention that three individuals from Sandia Pueblo—José María Moquino, Andres de la Candelaria, and Antonio de la Cruz—were in Mexico City a few days after Ramos and his unnamed companions approached the city on February 3, providing testimony regarding Sandia Pueblo boundaries. One can wonder if these were in fact Ramos's three unnamed companions. The date of their testimony, February 13, 1841, ten days after Ramos and his companions arrived on the outskirts of Mexico City, seems too much of a coincident to be otherwise.

Despite several unanswered questions, the document serves as a valuable voice from the past, allowing us to trace at least some of the route taken by these individuals on their mysterious trip to Mexico.

CHAPTER FIVE

The Cholera Epidemic of 1833

On August 9, 1833, Juan Felipe Ortiz, president of Santa Fe's ayuntamiento, reported to Governor Francisco Sarracino of a meeting held to discuss whether there was a need to quarantine a caravan of North American merchants under the command of Carlos (Charles) Bent to prevent or reduce the danger of contagion from cholera, a deadly disease caused by contaminated water. Ortiz indicated that the meeting could not achieve a consensus on what should be done and asked Sarracino for his opinion on the matter.

Although Governor Sarracino's response has not come to light, it is likely that the caravan was not kept under quarantine very long, if at all. A week before Ortiz reported the meeting, Charles Bent had communicated with presidio commander José M. Ronquillo, reassuring Ronquillo that although some of the goods in his wagons may have come from a ship that had transported some sick soldiers from New Orleans, no one on the caravan arriving in New Mexico was ill with cholera. The reason Bent provided this reassurance to Ronquillo is not clear although it may have been because New Mexico was well informed of the cholera epidemic and Ronquillo personally broached the issue with Bent.

The advance of cholera along the New Mexican frontier had its origins as early as the fall of 1831, when several communications from authorities in Mexico warned that cholera had been reported aboard ships recently arrived at ports in Mexico. These ships had already been quarantined but local officials were warned that they should begin taking appropriate precautions.

New Mexican officials noted receipt of these warnings as early as December 1831 and advised their superiors in Mexico that they were prepared to report any cases of cholera that showed up in New Mexico.

There is no direct evidence that cholera reached New Mexico in epidemic proportions at this time, although an examination of the burial records for Santa Fe and nearby communities may show otherwise. It is clear, however, that the contagion ravaged parts of Mexico and spread northward through Coahuila and Texas by 1832, killing thousands. In a February 28, 1833, letter, Governor Santiago Abreu responded to officials in Mexico confirming he had received notices of cholera in Chiapas but assured officials he was confident that the standards of personal and domestic cleanliness they had in place would prevent the contagion in New Mexico.

If New Mexico was in fact spared the ravages of the epidemic it may have been due to the early warnings the territory had received and the precautions they had taken. These precautions may be reflected in the January 1833 *Bando de Policía y buen gobierno* prepared by the Licenciado Antonio Barreiro for the ayuntamiento of Santa Fe. (A transcript and translation of this document is found in Marc Simmons's "Antonio Barreiro's 1833 Proclamation on Santa Fe City Government," in the June 1970 issue of *El Palacio*). These municipal regulations address several issues, including a section on public health and sanitation (*Salubridad*). The regulations required the draining of standing or stagnant pools of water, prohibited the fouling of rivers and irrigation ditches; regular cleaning of public streets and plazas; proper disposal and burning of trash and rubbish; prompt burial of cadavers; and the cleanliness and care of meats, grains, and flour prepared for human consumption.

The final section of health regulation establishes a *junta de sanidad* (health or sanitation bureau/committee) and in a late 1833 letter to his superiors in Mexico, Governor Sarracino acknowledged he had received information regarding the cholera epidemic and indicated that he had established juntas de sanidad as required by law in order to restrain foreigners, whom they feared could import the disease. It may have been one of these sanitation committees that debated whether to quarantine Charles Bent's caravan that summer of 1833.

It may be of special interest to students of herbal medicinal practices that local officials expressed great interest in several herbs that were reportedly effective in preventing or reducing the ravages of cholera. These included a suggestion by Governor Santiago Abreu that alcaldes should investigate the use of a *planta o medalla de cobre* (a copperleaf plant or copper medal that can be worn like an amulet) that was reported effective in preventing the contagion. Abreu also indicated that he had personally been using the herb *guaco,* and the diputación had asked the governor to send a sample of the herb to Mexico to see if anyone could confirm whether this was an effective treatment for cholera. Later that year, Governor Francisco Sarracino responded to the governor of the State of Chihuahua who had asked if the herb mariola was used in New Mexico as a treatment or remedy during the cholera epidemic. Sarracino indicated that he was not aware of its use locally and asked his counterpart in Chihuahua to send some samples with the next mail pouch so he could determine whether the plant was found in New Mexico.

CHAPTER SIX

Education During the Mexican Period

Education During the Mexican Period

The advent of Mexican independence in 1821 and the records of the Mexican Archives of New Mexico provide a substantial amount of information about education for that era. The earliest Mexican-period report of children attending school in Santa Fe comes from the records of the military garrison. An August 16, 1822 list of troops that had children in school shows that they paid tuition on a scale based on the individual military rank and salary of the father. Lieutenant José Caballero, for example, is listed with one child attending at six reales a month; cabos and carabineros paid four reales per child, while soldiers paid three reales. The sixty-two children listed in this report show that the unidentified teacher was paid a total of twenty-six pesos, one real, that month.

The issue of how to pay teachers was a continuous problem despite extraordinary efforts by New Mexico's officials to encourage education. One 1822 petition from the ayuntamiento of San Felipe detailed the need for a school and requested assistance to hire Ignacio Sánchez Vergara as a teacher. The diputación, however, responded that no funds were available, and that the residents of the pueblo were responsible for paying the teacher. The petition is not clear whether a school was in operation at that time in San Felipe or whether they were seeking funds to hire Sánchez so they could open a school.

Official efforts to establish public schools are reflected by an 1824 proposal to fund a principal teacher and an assistant at schools in the villas of Santa Fe, Santa Cruz de la Cañada, and Albuquerque. The committee assigned to appoint teachers at these schools, however, apparently did not do much to implement the proposal. The following year, a commission consisting of Antonio Sena, Juan Diego Sena, and Francisco Baca y Ortis pessimistically reported that the capital had no school "worthy of the name" and they found no one capable of directing one. The report sadly notes that parents demonstrated a profound lack of interest in education and concluded that parents seemed to feel that the raising of goats was the only skill children needed to learn. Despite orders and threats of local judicial officials, this resistance by parents often raised its ugly head whenever new schools were proposed or actually established. One such example was the proposed opening of a school at Algodones in 1826. As a list of children who could attend was being compiled, parents protested they did not have the resources to sustain the school. Such issues of funding and attendance plagued New Mexico's schools for decades.

Despite such problems, records of the diputación and local ayuntamientos clearly reflect the significant efforts, if not results, that went into the development and management of schools during this period. Several published and proposed regulations reflect what education may have been like in early nineteenth-century New Mexico. These cover the general philosophy of education, duties of teachers, discipline of students, and school terms and hours. Among these regulations is one article that directs each student to take a stick of wood to school to feed the fire during the winter months—the beginnings, possibly, of a practical tradition that continued in the memories of subsequent generations.

During subsequent years, a number of individuals—José Trinidad Barcelo, Vicente Sánchez Vergara, Manuel Echaverria (a controversial individual identified as "El Español"), Ignacio Ortiz, Teodoro (Teodocio?) Quintana, Marcelino Abreu, and Guadalupe Miranda are named as teachers at various schools during the Mexican period.

Schools continued to open and close periodically due to a chronic lack of funds. In 1844 Governor Manuel Armijo reported that no schools were operating in New Mexico for that reason. A later report indicated that New Mexico had no secondary schools for the same reason it had no primary ones—a lack of funds.

Such was the status of education in New Mexico as our Mexican period came to a close. However, after New Mexico became part of the United States in 1846, educational opportunities remained limited. Only one public school, located in Santa Fe, was reported in 1846. By 1860, however, four private and seventeen public schools reported thirty-three teachers providing instruction for an estimated enrollment of 600 to 1400 students in New Mexico.

In 1860 the territorial legislature had passed "An Act Providing Means for the Education of Children" that placed the Justice of the Peace from each precinct in charge of appointing a person from each community to teach children "the first rudiments of learning." The law made attendance at school mandatory and threatened parents with fines if they failed to comply but also allowed for a series of "valid excuses." Exemptions included children whose father decided that "necessity" required him to keep the child out of school to tend their flock of sheep and goats. It was the same story that had unfolded in the Mexican period. Under this system, nearly every child in the mostly rural, agricultural, and pastoral communities of New Mexico could be exempted from attending school. The more things changed the more they remained the same!

It should be noted that most of the material on education found in this chapter has been incorporated into the author's comprehensive and extensively annotated article on education during New Mexico's Mexican period, which has been published in the Spring 2024 issue of the *New Mexico Historical Review* under the title "El Primer y Principal Ramo."

An Early Report Card

While we have limited information about education in Spanish-era New Mexico, education was very important during the colonial process in Mexico and other parts of the Spanish Empire. In Mexico, for example, schools were established as early as 1524 to teach Latin, music, and academic subjects to native youth. One of these early schools was founded in 1532 on the outskirts of Mexico City in a town named Santa Fe. A university which educated many of New Spain's early leaders in science, law, medicine, and theology was functioning in Mexico by the middle of the sixteenth century.

Unfortunately, this extraordinary educational tradition did not translate well to colonial New Mexico, where there is little evidence of formal schools during the seventeenth and eighteenth centuries. Whatever education was obtained by the youth of this colony seems to have been through home schooling or in classes conducted at the missions operated by the Franciscan friars. There is some indication that the wealthy may have sent their children to be educated in Mexico and Europe.

The earliest evidence of public schools in New Mexico is from the early 1800s. During this period, local ayuntamientos were recruiting citizens who could read and write to serve as teachers in locations where the population could support a school. An 1808 document indicates that teachers were paid through a fee structure that charged parents two reales a month per student. If a family had two children in school, the fee, or tuition, was five pesos a year for the first two and one real per month for each subsequent child. Attendance was mandated for all boys under twelve years of age, but apparently education for girls was not provided, or at least not required.

Our archives do not show at what point schools were actually started in New Mexico, but by 1807, one report shows 460 students in attendance at several schools in El Paso and its neighboring pueblos. In an 1812 report, the presidio company from Santa Fe indicated that 78 of the soldiers' children attended *la escuela de primeras letras* (school of primary letters) and proudly noted that sixty of these children could read and eighteen were beginning to learn to write. That same year, however, the report of Pedro Pino to the Spanish Cortes indicated that this system provided a primary education only to the children of those who could afford to contribute to the salary of the teacher.

Significant gains in public education began after Mexico achieved its independence from Spain. It is clear by their writings that many New Mexicans felt education was important in building a strong country, and by 1827 formal regulations had been passed by the various ayuntamientos to manage a system of public schools. The regulations for the schools at Santa Fe and Santa Cruz de La Cañada provide a fascinating look at what education may have been like in nineteenth-century New Mexico.

The "Statutes for the Regulation of the general school of this said Villa of Santa Cruz de la Cañada for the year 1827," which are examined in the subsequent chapter, are the most elaborate and interesting of these surviving regulations. The suggested curriculum is heavily weighted toward the study and learning of *la doctrina* (church doctrine), prayers, and attendance at religious services.

A personal touch is provided by several documents that can easily be characterized as report cards. One such report from March 1830 is of the monthly examination of students at the public school in Santa Fe by Marcelino Abreú. He lists twelve students who demonstrated progress during that period. Some of the terminology used in this report has evaded a useful translation, so it must suffice to list only the names

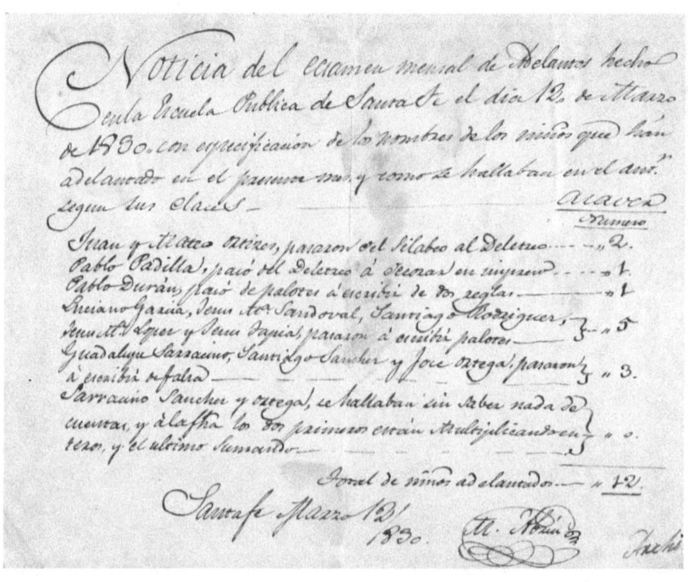

Noticia del examen mensal de adelantos hecho en la Escuela Publica de Santa Fe el día 12 de Marzo de 1830, con especificación de los nombres de los niños que han adelantado en el presente mes, y como se hallaban en el ant.r segun sus clases —

	Avanza Numero
Juan y Mateo Ortizes, pasaron del Silabeo al Deletreo	2.
Pablo Padilla, pasó del Deletreo á leer en impreso	1.
Pablo Durán, pasó de palotes á escribir de dos reglas	1
Luciano Garcia, Jesus M.a Sandoval, Santiago Rodriguez, Jesus M.a Lopez y Jesus Tapia, pasaron á escribir palotes	5
Guadalupe Sarracino, Santiago Sanchez y José Ortega, pasaron á escribir de falsa	3.
Sarracino Sanchez y Ortega, se hallaban sin saber nada de cuentas, y á la fha los dos primeros están Multiplicando entero, y el ultimo Sumando	0.
Total de niños adelantados	12.

Santa Fe Marzo 12/ 1830.

M. Abreú

Figure 21. "Noticia del examen . . ." Report of monthly examination, March 12, 1830. MANM: Legislative, 1830 Legislative, Ayuntamiento proceedings, jurisdiction of Santa Fe.

of the students here—Juan and Mateo Ortiz, Pablo Padilla, Pablo Duran, Luciano García, Jesús María Sandoval, Santiago Rodrigues, Jesús María Lopes, Jesus Tapia, Guadalupe Sarracino, Santiago Sanches, and José Ortega. Abreú noted that Sarracino, Sanches, and Ortega had entered school knowing nothing about numbers but could now do multiplications and sums. It can only be assumed that the parents of these children were as proud of them as any contemporary parent is of theirs.

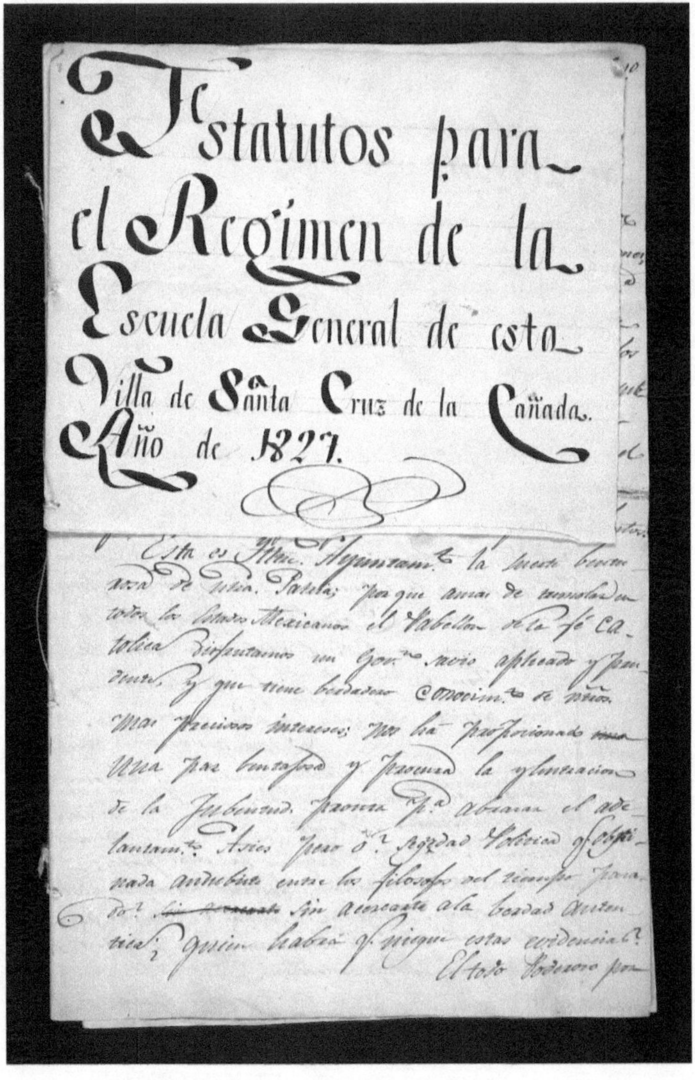

Estatutos para el Regimen de la Escuela General de esta Villa de Santa Cruz de la Cañada. Año de 1827.

Figure 22. Cover page, Regulations for the administration of the Santa Cruz de la Cañada school, May 25, 1827. MANM: 1827 Legislative, Ayuntamiento Proceedings.

School Regulations at Santa Cruz de la Cañada, 1827

The Mexican Archives of New Mexico contain a significant amount of information showing that local ayuntamientos and communities went to great lengths to establish and maintain schools during that period of our history. The May 25, 1827, "Estatutos para el regimen de la escuela de esta villa de Santa Cruz de la Cañada" (Statutes for the management of the school of this villa of Santa Cruz de la Cañada) is a wonderful document that reflects the era's general philosophy of education, duties of teachers, discipline of students, and school terms and hours.

The suggested curriculum is heavily weighted toward the study of *doctrina* (Church doctrine), civics, and attendance at religious services, a factor consistent with a document that has as its heading a line from Psalm 110, verse 8, in Latin and Spanish:

> *Initium Sapienta Timor Domini.*
> *El principio de la saviduría es el temor de Dios.*
> [The basis of knowledge is a fear of God.]

These regulations are divided into three principal sections. The first is a preamble that sounds more like a prayer than a statement. The second is a list of nine regulations regarding the management of the school, and the third section consists of fourteen items concerning the teacher's obligations. The school regulations are summarized as follows:

1. The school was to be located within the limits of the villa and main plaza and could not be relocated arbitrarily by the teacher or any local authority. The teacher was to be provided a house to live in and a hall appropriate to the needs of the school;
2. No teacher could be hired without a proper examination in reading, writing, and arithmetic (*contar*) and without the approval of the diputación. The teacher was also to demonstrate character and patriotism, and must appear before the local alcalde to swear to uphold the principles of the Holy, Catholic, Apostolic Roman Church;
3. The teacher could not leave the villa for any reason and was to have his permanent residence there on all workdays and Sunday mornings;
4. School was to open at six in the morning every day until nine, when the children were dismissed for half an hour to have their breakfast, then resume until noon, reopen at two, and remain open until six in the summer and five in the winter.
5. Children were to present themselves at school modestly attired and with clean faces and hands—so they would not soil the schoolbooks. Punishment for this infraction was three *palmetares* (slaps by the palm of the hand);
6. Every morning from six to nine was reserved for review or recitation of lessons from the previous afternoon; from two to four in the afternoon was a study period and every evening the teacher was to see that students recited lessons from the catechism in a loud and clear voice;

7. The children were to attend mass together every Sunday and festival day. The teacher was to march them from the school to church and make sure they demonstrated the proper devotion and respect required in the House of the Lord, which explains the earlier regulation that the teacher was to be present on Sunday mornings. On Thursdays, the principal lesson was from the Mexican constitution so that the children would grow in knowledge of citizenship and love for their country. Saturday mornings were reserved for lessons in the catechism;
8. The teacher was prohibited from whipping the children or using other "instruments of humiliation" or punishment which were prohibited by law and tended to frustrate the children. To discipline students, the teacher was to utilize moderate punishments proportional to the infraction, possibly as defined in item five above;
9. The teacher was to carefully instruct the children in the ways of good citizenship and to respect their elders and all ecclesiastical, civil, and military authority. No games were to be allowed in the playground that could be construed as being opposed to the virtues and morals of a good citizen, and the teacher was to see that students did not use inappropriate language;

These first nine sections were followed by more than a dozen rules for the teacher that were summarized in the final section, "The teacher shall treat the children with compassion, moderation, and paternal love, procuring for all their general improvement with no favoritism to some so there are no jealousies and rivalries among the children and their parents."

The elegantly written regulations were likely authored by Manuel de Jesús Rada, pastor at Santa Cruz, who reported the school had been dedicated to its spiritual patron San Juan de Nepomiceno. The patron saint's image was hung on the school wall alongside "the coat of arms of our immortal federal Mexican nation."

Padre Martínez's Proposal for Examination of Public School Teachers, 1831

According to the Santiago Valdez biography of the Reverend Antonio José Martínez, soon after Padre Martínez was appointed pastor of Our Lady of Guadalupe parish in Taos in November of 1826, he established a school for both sexes in his own house and hired and paid an unnamed teacher with his own funds to teach *primeras letras* (primary letters) to what Valdez called "these unenlightened people." Although Padre Martínez established and was funding his own primary school, indications are, the Taos ayuntamiento was seeking help from officials in Santa Fe to fund their own public school.

During this period, issues arose over the competency of teachers because an individual hired for the Taos public school had been found inept and was fired. In late 1830 three applicants for the position, Antonio Lucero, Francisco Varela, and Eulogio Valdes, were ordered to report to Santa Fe on January 16,

1831 so they could take a required examination. No document has surfaced that tells us what this examination consisted of, but during the January 1831 session of the diputación, Padre Martínez, who in addition to his clerical duties and maintaining his own school in Taos was also serving as a delegate to the council, submitted a proposal for the testing of students at the public schools. In the manner of many such proposals, it opens with a preamble,

> The Deputy (*Diputado*), here undersigned, desiring advancement of the elucidation of youth and who finds constancy in the good and complete learning on the part of the preceptors of the public schools of the territory, places before your Excellency the following proposition . . .

It then continues:

> As the acquisition of primary letters is the beginning (*principio*) of an elucidation that prompts men to progress in other levels of knowledge, patriotic sentiments, and of religion, benefiting society in general and each individual politically, civilly, and spiritually. At times the neglect of the Directors, or their failure to encourage the students, results in the detriment of discipline and imparts a bad example. I believe it useful and necessary that . . . by the end of this month or at the beginning of the next, each ayuntamiento where there is a public school . . . acquire information by means of a basic examination of what the students of that respective school have learned, such as to read, write, count, and know Christian doctrine by memory.

Martínez suggested the results of these examinations be archived for future reference so student progress could be monitored but also to determine if teachers were meeting their obligations. A committee assigned to review the proposal submitted its tacit approval and recommended it be forwarded to gefe politico José Antonio Chaves for submission to the ayuntamientos.

Unfortunately, Padre Martínez's proposal provides no details on what constituted student progress and teacher competency. In November 1830, shortly before Padre Martínez made his proposal, the diputación considered a recommendation by delegate Teodocio Quintana that all schools in the territory, except for the one in Santa Fe, be suspended or closed until a committee had completed the examination of every teacher who had been recommended or hired.

Quintana himself was a *maestro de escuela* (school teacher) in Albuquerque when he was considered for a teaching position in Santa Fe in 1827. When Quintana applied for the Santa Fe position, the diputación convened an extraordinary public session on August 9, 1827, to examine Quintana and Ignacio Ortiz, who apparently was the interim teacher. The examination may have been scheduled because the minutes of the session include a report that claimed Ortiz did not know "even the most essential" subjects. After hearing and dismissing an anonymous complaint regarding Quintana's ability to hold the position due to his debts, the council agreed to move into a "secret session" to consider whether the candidates could recite the *cinco reglas* (five rules) of accounting, which were apparently considered the basis of all teaching. While the documents do not tell us what these five rules of accounting were, Quintana reportedly recited the cinco reglas flawlessly while Ortiz was unable to respond to the challenge, although he claimed to know how to add, multiply, and pray. After the candidates were dismissed the council secretary officially notified Ortiz he was no longer the teacher and advised Quintana he was to assume the position, apparently immediately. Five days later, the diputación resolved to inform the governor of the vacancy created at the school in Albuquerque (presumably the one vacated by Quintana) and asked him to advise the ayuntamiento there to submit their nominations for teacher so they could arrange for an examination and hiring of the most qualified one.

Governor Albino Pérez's Proposal for Education, 1836

In July 1836, Governor Albino Pérez submitted a proposal to Santa Fe's ayuntamiento suggesting a commission be established to open and oversee three primary schools in Santa Fe. The first sections of Pérez's proposal concern themselves with issues related to the finding, hiring, paying, and examining of teachers in "reading, writing, and counting" to assure that candidates had "the best possible capabilities." Parents would be required to pay whatever was agreed to between the individual parents and the teacher, allowing parents to pay with *efectos de la tierra* (products of the land), which may have included crops, livestock, or even goods such as blankets or tanned hides. The poor and orphans were to be taught "free of charge."

All children aged five to twelve were required to attend one of the three schools. Those twelve and older would be required to take an apprenticeship with tradesmen from the "diverse branches of industry" so they could learn an occupation with which to make a living upon reaching adulthood. Children who did not apply themselves to learn a trade would be considered vagrants and sentenced to unspecified punishment by a tribunal that would be established for that purpose, probably like a contemporary juvenile court. Parents who resisted or refused to send their children to school were to be fined five pesos, with the fine doubling and tripling for subsequent violations. Those parents who were unable to pay the fine were subject to three days of arrest, with the time under arrest doubling and tripling, as in the monetary fines.

To enforce these regulations, appointed officials referred to as *alcaldes de barrio*, would have the authority to arrest youngsters twelve or older whom they found wandering the streets or in public places such as gambling houses, or attending other "bad entertainments," although the proposal does not specify what were considered bad entertainments. To effectively implement these regulations, each precinct was to have an appointed commissioner of public instruction who was tasked with preparing a list that included the name, age, and occupation of every citizen in their precinct. He was also obliged to keep a separate ledger listing all the children who were required to attend school as well as those youngsters who were apprenticed to a tradesman so the commissioner could determine if the apprentice was learning and progressing in the selected trade.

Parents of children not in compliance with the regulations were to be admonished "politely" up to three times before being reported to the alcaldes and punished according to the proposed regulations. Adults found "living in idleness" were to be admonished in an undefined manner and all "suspicious characters" were to be reported for unspecified actions.

Finally, the school commissioners and local alcaldes were to visit the schools and workshops every month and record in their ledgers anyone who might move into or leave their respective precincts. They were also to inspect and watch for the cleanliness of the streets and roads, reporting to the regidor de cano (council member on duty) of any that may need attention or repairs.

The extensive responsibilities assigned to these school commissioners and local alcaldes was deemed a "civic duty" with obligatory terms of six months. The possibility that the commissioners may have had a thankless and difficult job is suggested by final articles of the proposed regulations, which authorized a heavy fine of five to twenty-five pesos for "whomever insults the commissioner for doing his duty." On the other hand, while the threat of fines may have mitigated criticism or opposition, school commissioners found lacking "in the performance of their obligations" faced a stiff fine of ten to thirty pesos and removal from office. The proposal even suggests that there could be corruption in such a position and specified that if a school commissioner tolerated or covered up for "perverse men" by not reporting them to judicial officers, a heavy fine of fifty pesos or two months of public service could be applied.

Much of what Governor Pérez incorporates into his proposal suggests that he seemed to perceive that Santa Fe's residents, if not New Mexico as a whole, lacked industry and its citizens, motivation. The opening paragraphs to his proposal are an essay on the role of education in combating what he described as *olgasanería y la ociocidad*—an indolence and aversion to or lack of interest in work. In his view, the city's children wandered the streets like vagrants instead of being provided with the opportunity to acquire an education appropriate to their age. Consequently, they were regularly exposed to idleness and other vices, traits that were the cause of great evils to society and for which the simplest and most effective remedy was the education of the country's children.

The governor's ambitious plan, however, seems to have gone nowhere. A committee consisting of Blas Roibal, Antonio Sena, and Gaspar Brito reviewed the proposal and recommended the ayuntamiento implement the proposal in its entirety. They thanked the governor effusively for his many efforts on behalf of the territory, but there is no indication that the ayuntamiento acted on any element of the proposal.

CHAPTER SEVEN

Glimpses of Daily Life

One of Life's Tragedies, 1824

Within the thousands of documents in our Spanish and Mexican Archives are an equal number of stories. Many of these tell of the accomplishments of ancestors—some of them extraordinary; many of them quite ordinary. Some deal with extraordinary events while others tell only the dry facts of the lives they lived. They also point out that *mas antes* (in the old days), people also suffered their fair share of tragedy.

The story of one of these tragedies begins with the August 12, 1824, entry of a burial performed by Father Manuel Bellido, the parish priest of Taos. That day, Father Manuel laid to rest the body of a boy named José de Jesús Cordova. The burial record dutifully notes that José was the legitimate son of Serafino Cordova and Candelaria Medina but does not provide any details about the young man or his death. Within an unrelated set of documents found among the legislative records of the Mexican Archives of New Mexico, however, we find that José de Jesús was ten years old, deaf, and the victim of a rockslide that crushed him.

Details from these records reveal that on August 11, 1824, the alcalde of the barrio (neighborhood or settlement) of Arroyo

Seco reported to the alcalde mayor of Taos, José Gabriel Martínez, that a young boy had been killed. Since Martínez was on his way to Santa Fe on official business, he ordered the regidor, Bicente Trujillo, to convene an investigation and determine whether there were any suspicious aspects to the death.

On August 13, Trujillo appeared before the ayuntamiento of the Pueblo of Taos, accompanied by two boys, Francisco Barela, age eleven, and Antonio Martines, age ten. Both boys were with José de Jesús when he was killed. They testified that the three of them had been in the mountains gathering berries on that fateful day of August 11. Francisco indicated that he and Antonio had been walking along the edge of a cliff or steep hillside when he had stepped on a rock that came loose and began to roll down the hill. Antonio testified that he did not see the rock come loose but had heard the noise it made as it rolled down the hill. Neither was apparently aware that José was in the path of the falling rocks.

When the alcalde mayor, José Gabriel Martínez, returned to Taos from Santa Fe, he reviewed the testimony and filed his report which, he states, was based on "the written declarations as well as other verbal statements made by other citizens to my assistant and to me personally." He decided that Francisco could not possibly have thrown such large rocks on purpose, and that when Francisco stumbled, he had accidentally caused the rockslide that had struck and killed José de Jesús. The investigation also revealed that José, the victim, was deaf and unable to hear the rumbling of the rocks as they tumbled toward him, nor any warnings his companions may have shouted at him. Martínez concluded that the tragedy was the result of an unavoidable accident.

This portrait of one family's personal tragedy is made more interesting by a simple, one-page agreement between Juan Isidro Barela, Francisco's father, and Serafino Cordova, father of the boy who was killed. The document states that both parties agreed and understood that Cordova had no legal claim against Barela because the facts of the incident showed clearly that no one was at fault. However, the document says that *if* there had been some culpability on the part of Barela, Cordova forgave him and his family. In appreciation and grateful acknowledgment of that forgiveness, Barela agreed to pay José de Jesús's funeral expenses and gave Cordova a piece of property as compensation for the loss of his son.

This agreement between Cordova and Barela is the principal reason the archives in Santa Fe have detailed information on the boy's death. Unnamed officials in the capital had apparently wondered if the agreement had been part of a payoff or bribe to avoid criminal charges in a suspicious death. José Gabriel Martínez worded his concluding report in no uncertain terms, noting that he and the other local officials in Taos had followed the intent, if not the letter of the law and asked the unnamed officials in Santa Fe to "forgive whatever errors we may have committed, as they have been done . . . in good faith and . . . from our ignorance of such matters [of law]." Martínez signed off with a defiant flourish, noting, "this is all I have to say regarding this matter."

While these documents provide us with details surrounding the accidental death of a young boy in northern New Mexico, they also help us understand a family's tragic loss of a son and the guilt and sense of responsibility apparently felt by the parents of a young man who inadvertently caused the death of a friend.

CHAPTER SEVEN

A Power of Attorney, 1841

There is an interesting document in the 1841 judicial proceedings of the Mexican Archives of New Mexico that tells us several things about what was going on during that understudied and misunderstood period of our history. At first glance, it is a simple power of attorney, a contract dated May 19, 1841, between seven of the pueblos and Captain Miguel Antonio Lovato. The document is executed and witnessed by Lovato, Albino Chacón, Juan Bautista Vigil y Alarid, Francisco Tomás Baca, and Joaquin Chávez, some of the most prominent and well-known individuals of that time.

On that day in Santa Fe, Albino Chacón, who identified himself as the "second constitutional alcalde" of Santa Fe's municipal council, noted that Lovato and the "governors, generals, and principal men" of the seven following pueblos had appeared personally before him: San Juan, Santa Clara, San Yldefonso, Pojoaque, Nambe, Tesuque, and Sandia, "and . . . all said . . . that in the name of all the pueblos they represent and recognizing their right to give, as they do give, all their special and general power combined, full and complete, as in their right and worth, to the said Captain, who accepted it for all their suits, civil and government, current and pending."

There are several items that are significant in this document. First, it provides the names of many Pueblo officers at that moment in history. While it does not list all the pueblo officers from all nineteen New Mexico pueblos, it does provide important information for the seven Tewa pueblos with whom the contract was made. In the following list of pueblo officers present, the term abbreviated as "gral" in the document is probably a Spanish abbreviation for the position commonly known as the *capitán de guerra*, or "war captain" in pueblo government and listed here as "general."

San Juan: Santa Clara

Joaquin Castellano, governor
José Antonio Naranjo, governor
Juan José Archuleta, general
José Rayos (?) Naranjo, general
Antonio José Archuleta, general

San Yldefonso: Pojoaque

Asencio Peña, governor
Juan Ynosencio Tafoya, governor
Francisco Pino, general
Santiago Samora, general
Antonio Gabaldón, general
Ilario Trujillo, general
Diego Antonio Romero, general

Nambe: Tesuque

José Domingo Mulga, governor
José Rafael Suazo, governor
Juan José Tapia, general
José María Vigil, general

Sandia

Diego Ramos, governor
Mariano Candelaria, general
José María Moquino, general
José Ortiz, general
Juan Ylario Pajarito (office not listed)

The pueblos apparently entered into this contract with Miguel Antonio Lovato because the Spanish-era position of *protector de Indios* (protector of the Indians) did not exist during the Mexican period. Since the sixteenth century, the Spanish government had appointed individuals to that position to represent and assist the Indigenous peoples of the New World to negotiate through the Spanish legal system. According to Charles Cutter's book on the topic, *Protector de Indios in Colonial New Mexico 1659–1821*, the office was "designed to facilitate Indian participation in the judicial process . . . and often played a major role in aiding them in judicial matters." The position, however, was abolished with the Spanish constitution of 1820, which declared that all free men in the Spanish Empire were Spaniards, making the position unnecessary because the Native Americans were, in theory, "equal in all else to Spaniards." In New Mexico, the position was inconsistently filled through the late eighteenth and early nineteenth centuries. The last two *protectores* in New Mexico were Felipe Sandoval and Ignacio Sánchez Vergara. The lack of this official protection and legal assistance during the Mexican period may explain why the Tewas contracted with a private individual to provide legal representation. It is unknown if Lovato ever represented any of these seven pueblos in legal actions or suits.

Subsequent documents, however, show that Lovato apparently had similar contracts with other pueblos. On August 23, 1844, Lovato appears as the *apoderado*, or legal representative, of the Pueblo of Santo Domingo in their petition to Governor Mariano Martínez for a measurement of their pueblo league (see "Measuring the Santo Domingo Pueblo League, 1844" p. 78).

Cinco de Mayo

Every year, as the fifth of May approaches, merchants throughout the nation begin to advertise Mexican-themed sales of everything from automobiles and furniture to specials on the chile, tortillas, and other ethnic foods associated with Cinco de Mayo celebrations. Many communities and civic organizations sponsor festivals that feature parades, music, dancing, and food. A Google search for the topic reveals hundreds of Cinco de Mayo celebrations throughout the nation—from Portland, Oregon, Atlanta, Georgia, and St. Paul, Minnesota, to the "Fruitvale Festival and Parade" held that day in Oakland, California. Even the White House has a formal celebration, and you can purchase a dark-haired "Cinco de Mayo Barbie Doll" that comes with a colorful Mexican costume!

However prevalent these celebrations are today, they are a relatively recent phenomenon in New Mexico. Despite widespread, enthusiastic participation in these festivities, most are unaware of the actual historical significance of the events they are celebrating.

Cinco de Mayo is not, as often portrayed, the Mexican Fourth of July. It emerged as a Mexican holiday after Mexican General Ignacio Zaragoza defeated a French army at Puebla on May 5, 1862. Earlier that year, Napoleon III, taking full advantage of a United States preoccupied with a bloody civil war, embarked on an ambitious plan to conquer Mexico and expand the French colonial empire in the Caribbean. The French expected to easily overthrow the Mexican government, headed by Benito Juárez, but soon after French troops landed at Vera Cruz and began their march toward Mexico City, they encountered unexpected fierce resistance at Puebla.

By military standards, Zaragoza's defeat of the French was a small victory. The French soon succeeded in their short-lived conquest of Mexico, and Napoleon installed the Austrian archduke, Ferdinand Maximilian, as emperor of Mexico. When the US civil war ended in 1865, the American government asserted its policy of opposing European interference in the Western hemisphere under the Monroe Doctrine and pressured France to end its occupation of Mexico. By 1867 France began to withdraw its forces, and Maximilian was captured by troops of the Mexican Republic. He was executed by a firing squad on June 19, 1867.

For Mexicans, their victory over the French at Puebla was a tremendous moral victory that has been commemorated annually since Mexico succeeded in expelling the French in 1867. On May 3, 1867, a printed broadside issued by Juan Nepomuceno Méndez, the interim governor and military commander of the "Free and Sovereign State of Puebla," proclaimed a formal "national festival consecrated to the memory of the glorious event that occurred in the suburbs of this city, when the armed forces and Mexican people under the command of the illustrious General Ignacio Zaragoza, stood victorious over the French."

Cinco de Mayo commemorates events that took place nearly two decades after the United States occupied New Mexico in 1846, yet there is some evidence of local observance of the festival in New Mexico during the late nineteenth century. Research by Anselmo Arellano suggests that northern New Mexicans took advantage of special excursion trains in the late 1800s to visit cities in Mexico in time to celebrate Cinco de Mayo. In 1892 La Estrella Literaria (Literary Star), a Las Vegas intellectual and educational organization, hosted a dance to commemorate the holiday. Arellano attributes local support and observation of these Mexican patriotic events to lingering familial and emotional ties that many New Mexicans retained to their mother country after New Mexico was annexed by the United States through the Treaty of Guadalupe Hidalgo in 1848. Arellano, however, found little evidence that New Mexicans celebrated Cinco de Mayo very much in the early twentieth century except in southern New Mexico communities that had a concentration of more recent Mexican immigrants.

That, however, has changed in recent decades. A growing awareness of New Mexico's Mexican heritage as well as significant increases in Mexican immigration has prompted an explosion of Cinco de Mayo celebrations nationwide. One can understand that Goliad, Texas, the birthplace of General Zaragoza, who defeated the French in 1867, would honor this local hero every fifth of May. But Hawaii? Surprisingly, a major Cinco de Mayo celebration is held annually in Kona, Hawaii, by descendants of Mexican vaqueros (cowboys) from California who migrated to Hawaii in the 1830s to work and train Hawaiians in the livestock industry.

While Cinco de Mayo has emerged recently as a significant festival throughout the United States, it remains essentially a Mexican celebration that has little historical basis for observation in New Mexico. There is, however, another Mexican celebration that has a long, if interrupted, tradition in New Mexico. As noted in the subsequent chapter, New Mexicans enthusiastically celebrated the real Mexican equivalent of the American Fourth of July—*16 de septiembre.*

Santa Fe's Grand 1844 Celebration of Mexican Independence

Many documents in the Mexican Archives of New Mexico have been a personal revelation. Among these are those that have shown that New Mexicans observed 16 de septiembre, the traditional date of Mexican independence, with the same fervor of any patriotic Mexican citizen.

I first pointed out these local celebrations of Mexican independence in a September 1997 "Voices From the Past" column and continued research into the topic resulted in a full chapter on "Mexican Patriotism in New Mexico, 1821–1846," appearing in *Telling New Mexico: A New History*, which was published by the Museum of New Mexico Press in 2009. Of all the material

I have seen on the topic over the years, those describing Santa Fe's 1844 celebration of 16 de septiembre make it clear that city officials expected to have one of the most elaborate celebrations ever held in the capital.

A bundle of documents in our Mexican Archives describes an elaborate program organized by a commission composed of twenty-nine of Santa Fe's most distinguished residents. The commission's first meeting was held on July 28, 1844, to begin planning for "the celebration of the anniversary of our glorious Independence." As commissions are apt to do, their first action was to organize subcommittees and assign them specific responsibilities. One was assigned to plan for refreshments, another to arrange for public entertainment, a third to meet with the governor and military authorities to arrange for military salutes, and another to meet with church officials and arrange for various religious ceremonies.

The refreshment committee prepared a list of what they considered "indispensable" to serve at the dance planned for the 16th. The planned refreshments were a tantalizing assortment of pastries—*marquesotes, puches, coronas, soletas, encaladillas,* dulces, and *biscochos de regalo*—with the ingredients listed for each item, in the event anyone might be interested in duplicating the treats. Liquid refreshments were budgeted at seventy-four pesos for forty-three flasks of wine and twenty-five of aguardiente, which were going into the punch.

The most detailed recommendations were submitted by the entertainment committee who planned to open the celebration the night of September 15 with a serenade and a speech by Santa Fe's alcalde, don Tomás Ortiz. At eleven that evening, a

Lista de los Ciudadanos nombrados p.r el E. S. Gober-nador p.a componer la Junta Patriotica á fin de q.e determine de la Celebridad del Aniversario de nuestra gloriosa Independencia, reunida en 28 de Julio de 1.844. p.a el lustre del dia 16. de Setiembre de dicho año: asaver.

Sr. Cura Vicario
Dn. Juan Felipe Ortiz. 1.
Sr. Coronel D. Pedro Muñoz, en seg.da finado. 1.
Sr. D. Felipe Sena. 1.
Sr. D. Antonio Sena. 1.
Sr. D. [illegible]. 1.
Sr. D. Francisco Ortiz, y Baca 1.
Sr. D. Donaciano Vigil.. 1.
Sr. D. Juan Baut.a Vigil. 1.
Sr. D. Tomas Ortiz 1.
Sr. D. Fran.co Ortiz y Delg.do 1.
Sr. D. Fran.co Baca y Ort.z 1.
Sr. D. Benito Larragoiti. 1.
Sr. D. Juan [illegible].. 1.
Sr. D. Justo Pino .... 1.
Sr. D. Santiago Flores 1.
Sr. D. Santiago Armijo.. 1.
Sr. D. Seraf.n Ramirez 1.
Sr. D. Ant.o Sena Rivera 1.
Sr. D. Ant.o José Rivera 1.
Sr. D. Agustin Duran 1.
Sr. D. Ant.o Matias Ortiz 1.
Sr. D. Feliz Zubia... 1.
Sr. D. Nicolas Pino.. 1.
Sr. D. Miguel Pino... 1.
Sr. D. José Abreu 1.
Sr. D. Bern.do Vazq.z Franco 1.
Sr. D. Fran.co Martinez 1.
Sr. Cura D. Fran.co Leiba 1.
Sr. D. Ig.o M.a Flores 1.
En 28. de Julio de 1844: q. son — 29.

Se rebaja el Sr. Coronel D. Pedro Muñoz p.r haber muerto el dia 30 del mismo Julio — 1

Total 28

Santa Fe Julio 28. de 1.844.

Bernardo Vazquez Franco
Secretario

Figure 22. List of citizens selected to plan the 1844 16th of September celebration. Proceedings of Junta Patriotica, July 28, 1844. MANM: 1844 Miscellaneous.

general ringing of bells, and a salvo of artillery and fireworks would begin the celebration. These activities were to serve "as a joyous remembrance of the moment at which the immortal Hidalgo proclaimed our National Independence at the Pueblo of Dolores."

At dawn on the 16th, a troupe of musicians would open festivities in front of the palace, followed by an artillery salute and a general ringing of church bells as the national flag was unfurled. At seven, masses would be celebrated in all the chapels of the city, and at nine, the governor, accompanied by the city's civil and military officials, would proceed to the parish church for another mass and Te Deum. The governor would then lead all the attending dignitaries in a procession to the plaza where they were to install the cornerstone of a monument that was being erected to commemorate Mexican independence.

On the afternoon of the 16th, the military band would provide music while *volarines* and *maromeros* (acrobats) entertained along the street. That evening at eight, fireworks would be followed by a series of public dances, one of which was to be held in the sala (hall) of the palace. The morning of the 17th, a solemn memorial mass was scheduled to honor all who had died for their country, followed by *corridas de toros* (bullfights) on the plaza, which would be fenced for the occasion.

The final report of this commission was submitted to the governor on October 13, 1844, by commission president Juan Felipe Ortiz and secretary Bernardo Vasquez Franco. There is no indication of how many of the planned activities were actually carried out, but intervening events suggest the possibility that the 16th of September celebration described by this report was not as grand as the commission envisioned.

On September 5, 1844, a band of Utes entered the capital to meet with Governor Mariano Martínez to discuss grievances related to a campaign against the Navajos the previous year. On the morning of September 6, the contentious meeting deteriorated into a general melee in which a Ute chief and several of his men were killed. This incident undoubtedly caused a great deal of concern and disruption in the capital, but there is no indication of whether these events interfered with plans for the celebration of Mexican independence scheduled to take place ten days later. Orders issued to the garrison troops for the 15th and 16th confirm that honor guards and escorts were formed consistent with the plans described in the 1844 Junta Patriotica documents. It may be that while the clash with the visiting Utes moderated some of the plans, it apparently it took more than an attack on the capital to disrupt a good fiesta in New Mexico.

Welcoming the Bishop

New Mexico endured many conflicts between the Catholic Church and government officials during its colonial history. Despite these conflicts, the Church worked closely with the Spanish and Mexican governments in many aspects of daily life. Officers and troops of the presidio in Santa Fe were often called upon to participate in the many ecclesiastical celebrations observed throughout the year.

The men and officers of the presidio were often on duty that was dangerous. Spanish- and Mexican-era records show that presidio troops were assigned to deliver the mail pouch to El Paso del Norte, guard the horse herd, and escort caravans that went south to Chihuahua as well as the American commercial caravans from the United States. They were often stationed at frontier outposts such as San Miguel del Bado, Jémez, Abiquiú, Ojo Caliente, Cebolleta, and Sevilleta. These men were also on seemingly endless campaigns against the Comanches, Apaches, Navajos and Utes. Some months, fewer than a dozen troops were present and available for duty at the garrison itself.

The monotony of garrison duty and the dangers of service were thankfully interrupted by other activities. Troops were often assigned as honor guards for civic and religious services. During the Mexican period, troops were naturally an integral part of the annual 16th of September celebrations and the ayuntamiento of Santa Fe regularly invited the commanding officer of the presidio and his men to participate in Holy Week activities. The general orders for April 11–12, 1838, for example, assign all soldiers not on guard or garrison duty to serve as an honor guard for the Blessed Sacrament on Holy Thursday and Good Friday. Holy Week activities included ceremonies during which weapons and flags were veiled and drums muffled during religious services.

Of all the preparations for these civic and religious celebrations, it is likely that none were more elaborate and anticipated than episcopal visits from the Bishop of Durango. Of several such *visitas* to New Mexico none are better documented than the 1760 visitation by don Pedro Tamarón y Romeral (the first since Bishop Benito Crepo's visita of 1730). Making his way north from El Paso del Norte in early May of 1760, Tamarón must have been accompanied by an impressive retinue. The Eleanor B. Adams translation of his journal tells us that when preparations for his departure from New Mexico were being made later that summer, the bishop's escort consisted of 21 soldiers and 55 militia, 429 horses and mules, 28 bulls, and 450 sheep. The entire group consisted of a total of 94 people, including 17 who were likely Tamarón's personal staff.

As Tamarón made his way north along the camino real, he made his first episcopal visits at Tomé, Albuquerque, and Sandia, where he was met by an escort of twenty soldiers and an officer from the presidio in Santa Fe. A short distance north of the Pueblo of San Felipe, Bishop Tamarón was met by Governor Marín del Valle in a light, two-seated carriage that the governor had made available for the bishop's use. Tamarón arrived in Santa Fe on May 24 and over the next several weeks, toured all of New Mexico's missions and towns except for Zuni before departing for New Mexico on July 8. While he was in Santa Fe, Tamarón described participation of the military garrison during the celebration of Corpus Christi at the capital. His understated description of the occasion notes that "the street through which the procession passed was decorated with branches and splendid altars; there were salvos by the military squadron, and a large crowd was present."

The next episcopal visitation to New Mexico was by Bishop José Antonio Laureano de Zubiría in 1833, but it is not as well documented as Zubiría's subsequent visita of 1845. New Mexico received news of the 1845 visitation in early February of that year.

As the bishop approached Santa Fe in mid-May, correspondence between vicar Juan Felipe Ortiz and the military commander demonstrates some excitement about the unspecified preparations that were being made for the bishop's arrival in Santa Fe. Presidio orders for June 11–12, 1845, indicate that the troops were to form in front of the Palace of the Governors to formally receive the bishop. To make the best possible presentation for the visiting prelate, the troops were ordered to wear their dress uniforms—their *vestidos de gala*—the only time I have seen the term used.

However impressive the sight of the presidio troops in the dress uniforms may have been that day, the color guard that formed for Bishop Zubiría in 1845 may have been one of the last times these troops participated in such civic or religious occasions. Little more than a year after Zubiría's departure from New Mexico, the US Army under General Stephen Watts Kearny occupied Santa Fe and the presidio was unceremoniously disbanded—its century and a half of service was forgotten and its role in our many religious celebrations faded from our memory.

Contract for a Horse Race, 1846

If we look at the official records of government during the spring of 1846, it was certainly an anxious time in New Mexico. Tensions were mounting between the United States and Mexico, and news from the capital in Mexico City warned of the necessity to begin preparations for war between the two nations. Despite the tensions and fears that such news undoubtedly brought, when we look beyond the rhetoric of politicians, we find that life went on. It was spring, and preparations had to be made to clean the acequias and plow the fields for another season of planting; livestock had to be tended and after a hard winter, maybe even some plans were made to enjoy life a little.

One seemingly insignificant document that illustrates how life went on during these difficult times is a formal contract for a horse race entered into by the Pinos of Santa Fe and Francisco Tomás Cabesa de Baca of Peña Blanca. The document, dated March 18, 1846, was prepared by Trinidad Barcelo, second constitutional alcalde of Santa Fe and is found in the 1846 judicial proceedings of the Mexican Archives of New Mexico. The following is my translation of the contract.

> In the city of Santa Fe, capital of the Department of New Mexico, on the 18th of March of 1846, before me the citizen Trinidad Barcelo, 2nd constitutional alcalde and my assisting witnesses with whom I am acting as delegated judges due to the lack of public scribes (of whom there are none in the territory), appeared personally the citizens Justo Pastor Pino and Miguel E. Pino of this city, whom I certify that I know personally as free men and gentleman of means, and these say:
>
> The later of whom I named, with authorization from the citizen Francisco Tomás Cabesa de Baca of Peña Blanca, has contracted with the first named and he with the other, a horse race, that they state is to take place the upcoming Sunday from nine to eleven of the day, for the distance of 500 Castilian varas, on firm and level ground and expressed that the site of the designated race [is to be] on the plain (*el llano*) of the wagon road that runs near [or by] the house of the late don Salvador Martín toward los Alamitos;

And that the horses in the race are the black (*prieto*) belonging to Justo Pastor Pino with the red (*colorado*) named "*mala ralla* (bad streak or lightning)" of don Francisco Tomás Cabesa de Baca and that the wager is ten bred heifers, new and without lesions, to be turned over by the one who loses to the winner by the first day of May of the current year, to which they agree, as well as 206 yards of cloth to be turned over to the winner by the loser at the end of the race; that the riders shall be of equal weight and only if either of the horses falls ill or other legal contingency, from today to the hour of the race, shall justify cancellation of the race; if none of these apply, the one who does not run shall be responsible for the value of the contract as if the race had been run.

To assure all is valid and secure, it is stipulated in the present document to the national justices that recognize the legality of the present business, and principally those of this city so they may compel compliance before competent authority without appeal.

As such the gentlemen Justo Pastor Pino and Miguel Estanislado Pino certify before me, and they ask that in order to properly validate the present security I authorize the same, so I the referred to Alcalde (as the parties ask), say that I so authorize with the faculties with which I am conferred, signing it with the parties and assisting witnesses with whom I certify, on this 18th day of March of 1846.

Signed: Trinidad Barcelo As assistants: Manuel Baca y Delgado

Justo Pastor Pino Calletano Garcia

Miguel E. Pino

The historical record does not tell us if the race was ever held. If the race was held, however, it would have been a greatly anticipated and well-attended event. Horses have long been valued commodities in New Mexico and anyone who boasted of blood lines or the speed of his horse would certainly have been challenged by another who was certain that his horse was faster.

It is too bad we do not know if the race was held and who won. Imagine all the side bets that would have been made on the hometown favorite and the heated discussions about the various attributes of each horse. One can visualize the cheering and exhortations of the crowd that lined the raceway and the inevitable disputes sparked by a close finish, arguments about fair starts, or violations of some unwritten rules. One cannot help but wish we had been there to witness this small but wonderful moment in New Mexico's past.

CHAPTER EIGHT

An Ignominious End

Searching for the Invader

It is not clear at what point New Mexico's government officials received official notice that a state of war existed between the United States and Mexico. By June 6, 1846, Governor Manuel Armijo had warned local officials of impending trouble based on information received from Mexican officials about the John Slidell mission. Slidell's mission took place before the May 13 declaration of war, so by then, Armijo's circular had warned New Mexico's citizens that war seemed inevitable and ordered local officials to prepare an inventory of arms and weapons and develop a list of the militia that would be available to defend the territory.

Documents in the Mexican Archives of New Mexico make it clear that the weeks preceding the actual entrance of US troops into Mexican territory were a flurry of activity, much of it associated with preparations for defense and the search for reliable intelligence of where the Americans were at the moment. On June 10 Antonio Baca reported from Anton Chico that José de la Cruz Aragón had encountered some foreigners presumed to be Americans at Los Esteros, and Francisco Segura and three men were sent to find and bring them to San Miguel del Bado. This group of eleven foreigners had no pack train with them so they were presumed to be spies for an approaching

US invasion and were escorted to Santa Fe to be interrogated by the governor.

The information these foreigners provided was apparently enough to prompt Armijo, as governor as well as military commander, to order detachments of troops from the Santa Fe, Taos, and San Miguel del Bado companies to scout along the northern frontier to the Rio Colorado for signs of the approaching US Army.

Only one report of these scouts has surfaced. A *Diario de Novedades* (Diary of Daily Occurrences) submitted by Captain Francisco Ortiz covers the period June 12 through July 1, 1846. Ortiz tells us that his expedition, which consisted of eight soldiers and two cabos, left San Miguel del Bado on Friday, June 12 "for the scout of the Rio Colorado" and for the first several days, scouted along the Cañon de los Apaches (Apache Canyon), to Pecos and Gusano, all sin novedad. On the 17th, they expanded the scout to Tecolote and Las Vegas, where they rested for two days and purchased two rams to feed the troops. They then proceeded to la Junta de Los Rios, north along the Gallinas River, and by June 23, arrived at Santa Clara (Wagon Mound), where they encountered an American merchant caravan, but otherwise recorded nothing noteworthy.

Frederick Adolph Wislizenus, in his *Memoir of a Tour to Northern Mexico*, noted that on June 23 the relatively large caravan he was traveling with encountered a troop of about thirty Mexican soldiers camped at the Santa Clara spring. He described it as the usual escort sent from Santa Fe or San Miguel del Bado to meet the merchant caravan and prevent smuggling. The Mexican soldiers Wislizenus encountered, however, must not have been Captain Francisco Ortiz and his men. The Ortiz scouting expedition was much smaller, and their orders stated specifically that they were to scout the Rio Colorado, not provide a caravan escort. It is puzzling that Ortiz did not mention other Mexican forces at Santa Clara.

For the next several days Captain Ortiz and his men retraced their route from Santa Clara down the Gallinas to La Junta and Las Vegas, all "sin novedad." On the 27th, the scout left Las Vegas and proceeded to Bernal and Gusano before arriving at Pajarito and Los Terrones, where they encountered a cabo named Servín, with whom Ortiz seems to have argued, calling him "insolent." Captain Ortiz arrived at Santa Fe on July 1, having scouted much of northeast New Mexico, and found nothing worthy of mentioning. His report seems strangely incomplete, considering he was supposed to try and find signs of an approaching American army. There is also no indication in the report why Captain Ortiz returned from the Santa Clara spring on June 24 instead of continuing north to the Rio Colorado, as per his orders. Did he learn something of importance about the location of General Kearny's forces from someone in the merchant caravan and felt it necessary to return to Santa Fe? If so, he certainly did not rush back to Santa Fe with any such information.

It is clear from Governor Armijo's correspondence that he received news that war had been declared between the United States and Mexico sometime before June 17. That day, Armijo sent a circular to the prefects advising that mail had arrived with the US merchant caravan that confirmed hostilities had broken out between the two countries, and that a force of Texans or Americans was approaching along the Rio Pecos. He ordered the prefects to organize all able-bodied men, exempting only the elderly and disabled, and to prepare to march on the governor's orders. The die had been cast. The American army would soon cross into Mexican territory and New Mexico's history would soon change forever.

Juan Bautista Vigil y Alarid Speech

On August 18, 1846, nearly two centuries ago, General Stephen Watts Kearny and his Army of the West occupied Santa Fe without firing a shot. Governor Manuel Armijo had, the day before, fled south to Chihuahua. In the midst of what must have been an extraordinarily chaotic and distressing day for the residents of the city, Juan Bautista Vigil y Alarid was among the New Mexicans who stepped forward to face Kearny and deal with an uncertain future.

The following is my English translation of the speech Vigil y Alarid delivered to General Kearny on August 19, 1846. The original Spanish manuscript is found in the William G. Ritch Papers at the Huntington Library in San Marino California.

> My Lord General: The discourses your Excellency has delivered in taking possession of this county in the name of the United States of North America provide us an idea of the glorious future that awaits us. The question of deciding the boundaries of Nations does not fall to us—the cabinets of Mexico and Washington will decide their differences. To us falls the duty to obey and respect the established authorities

Figure 24. "Raising American Flag Over Old Palace," August 18, 1846. Twitchell, *History of the Military Occupation*, 66.

despite our personal opinions. The sincere, honorable, and hardworking inhabitants of this Department offer their deference to the Government of North America. No one in this world has successfully resisted the power of the stronger. Your Excellency, do not think it strange that we have not manifested joy and enthusiasm in seeing our city occupied by your military forces. To us the political entity of the Mexican Republic has died. She, regardless of her circumstances, was our Mother. What son does not shed copious tears at the tomb of his parents? I could note some of the causes from whence came her dishonor, but domestic shortcomings should not be made public.

Suffice it to say that a civil war is the unfortunate cause of the deadly poison that has spread over one of the best countries that has come from the hands of the Creator. Today we belong to a great and powerful Nation. The stars and stripes [that fly over] your command tent spread across the horizon of New Mexico: Its resplendent light spreads across this country like seed sown and cultivated on fertile land. We recognize by the moderation [demonstrated] by your Lordship, by the manners of your accommodating officers, and by the rigorous discipline of your troops, that we belong to the Republic that owes its origins to the immortal Washington, who is admired and respected by all civilized Nations. How different our fate would have been, had we been invaded by the European Nations. We know what the unfortunate Poles are enduring!

In the name, then, of all the Department, I present obedience to the Republic of the North and offer to obey and respect its laws and authorities. Santa Fe, August 19, 1846

Juan Bautista Vigil y Alarid, Governor.

How did it fall to him to deliver this speech and why did Vigil y Alarid attach the title of "Governor" to his elegant signature and rubric? It is well documented that Vigil y Alarid was the secretary of government at that fateful moment in our history. This was a significant position in the Mexican government, but it was not, as has been suggested, the equivalent of being lieutenant governor or second in command. In the governor's absence, civil authority under the Mexican system was assumed

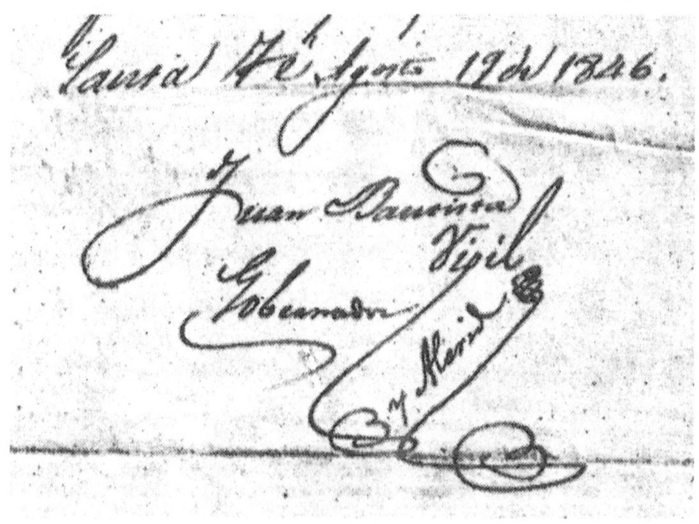

Figure 25. Juan Bautista Vigil y Alarid signature as governor, August 19, 1846. Twitchell, *History of the Military Occupation*, 77.

by the primer vocal of the territorial council. So how did he end up with the title?

One explanation is that Vigil y Alarid, likely the senior Mexican government official present in Santa Fe when the city was occupied, was appointed to the position by Kearny himself. In his memoirs, Philip St. George Cooke noted that Kearny appointed "temporary civil officers" on August 19, the same day Vigil y Alarid delivered his famous speech. However, the scant documentation of those hectic days does not specify who these "temporary civil officers" might have been.

Vigil y Alarid's term as governor, whether actual or self-appointed, was short-lived. On September 22, little more than a month after Kearny entered the city, Charles Bent was appointed governor. Following the Treaty of Guadalupe Hidalgo, Vigil y Alarid was among the several hundred New Mexicans who repatriated to Mexico. Research by my colleague Samuel Sisneros shows that Vigil y Alarid was active in the northern Chihuahua community of Guadalupe through the 1850s. By 1860 he returned to New Mexico and provided important expert testimony in support of community land grant claims before the US surveyor general.

At a time of great crisis, Juan Bautista Vigil y Alarid stepped to the forefront and became immortalized with some of the most poignant and heartfelt words ever uttered in New Mexico history. One day someone will examine the full and extraordinary life of this civic leader and Mexican patriot.

A Deceptive Silence

The August 1846 occupation of New Mexico by General Stephen Watts Kearny and the American Army of the West is usually characterized as "a bloodless conquest." For better or worse, Governor Manuel Armijo's decision to abandon the defenses at Apache Canyon and order his troops and militia to disperse enabled the occupation by American military forces to be accomplished without firing a shot. However, the bloody events of January 1847, which have become commonly known as the "Revolt of 1847," belie the notion of a "bloodless conquest."

Soon after the American army marched into Santa Fe, General Kearny issued a proclamation that warned the citizens

AVISO.

HALLANDOME debidamente antorizado por el Presidente de los Estados Unidos de America, por la presente hago los Siguientes nombramientos para la gobernacion de Nuevo Mejico, Territorio de los Estados Unidos.

Los Empleados asi nombrados seran obedecidos y respetados segun corresponde.

CARLOS BENT Será GOBERNADOR,
Donaciano Vigil " Secretario del Territorio,
Ricardo Dallum " Esherif mayor (alguacil
Francisco P. Blair" Promotor fiscal, [mayor)
Carlos Blumner" " Tesorero
Eugenio Leitensdorfer " Ytendente de cuentas públicas,

Joab Houghton, Antonio José Otero y Càrlos Beaubien seran Jués de la Suprema Cortede Justicia y cada uno en su Districto sera jues de circuito.

Dado en Santa Fé capital del terri de Nuevo Mejíco este dia á 22 de de Setiembre 1846, y el 71 ° de la Indepeneia de los Estados Unidos.

S. W KEARNY,
General de Brigada
del Egercito de los E. Unidos.

NOTICE.

BEING duly authorized by the President of the United States of America, I hereby make the following appointments for the Government of New Mexico, a territory of the United States.

The officers thus appointed will be obeyed and respected accordingly.

CHARLES BENT to be Governor.
Donaciano Vigil " Sec. of Territory.
Richard Dallam " Marshall.
Francis P Blair " U. S. D. A.'y
Gharles Blummer " Treasurer.
Eugene Leitensdorfer " Aud. of Pub. Acc.

Joal Houghton, Antonio Josè Otero, Charles Beaubien to be Judges of "the Superior Court."

Given at Santa Fe, the Capitol of the Territory of New Mexico, this 22d day of September 1846 and in the 71st year of the Independence of the United States.

S. W. KEARNY,
Brig. General
U. S. Army.

Figure 26. *Aviso/Notice*, S. W. Kearny, appointment of Territorial officers, September 22, 1846. Myra Ellen Jenkins and J. Richard Salazar, *Calendar to Microfilm Edition of the Territorial Archives of New Mexico* (State of New Mexico Records Center and Archives, 1974). Records of the Territorial Governors, 1846–1912: Military Occupation, 1846–1850, Stephen Watts Kearny, Proclamations.

of New Mexico that any resistance would be "foolish, ignorant and downright insanity . . ." As a precaution, Kearny disarmed the Mexican presidio companies at Santa Fe, Taos, and San Miguel del Bado, and ordered them to turn in their weapons and ammunition. Kearny also took steps to establish a civil government under the new American regime and on September 22, 1846, appointed several officials and judges, including Charles Bent to be governor, and Donaciano Vigil as secretary of the territory.

Figure 27. Charles Bent. Twitchell, *History of the Military Occupation*, 85.
Figure 27a. Donaciano Vigil. Twitchell, *History of the Military Occupation*, 206.

Kearny then issued the *Laws of the Territory of New Mexico*, the codification of American law that is more commonly known as the Kearny Code. With the new civil government in place, all seemed quiet in New Mexico and while war still raged in Mexico, the former Mexican territory of New Mexico appeared to be under peaceful occupation. Kearny, after touring the rio abajo, reported that New Mexico's inhabitants were "fully satisfied" with the change of government and confident there was no organized resistance, prepared to leave New Mexico in late September in command of three hundred dragoons headed to California.

But the silence was deceptive. In the late fall of 1846, reports surfaced of individuals who were speaking out against the occupation and encouraging resistance, if not revolt. It was becoming clear that many New Mexicans still considered themselves loyal Mexican citizens and felt that Donaciano Vigil and other supporters of the American government were collaborators and traitors.

By mid-December, Governor Bent reported that a faction headed by Diego Archuleta and Tomás Ortiz were trying to "excite" the citizens of New Mexico against the American government and several men suspected of a "conspiracy" to overthrow the new government were arrested. These arrests apparently stymied an uprising originally planned for the night of December 19, 1846.

Details are scarce, but despite these arrests, planning for a general uprising continued. On January 19, 1847, the home of Governor Bent at Don Fernando de Taos was attacked and Bent and several officials of the recently organized civil government were killed. Within days the uprising had spread through much of northern New Mexico, and several Americans and Mexican citizens supportive of the new government were killed.

In Santa Fe, Colonel Sterling Price received word of Governor Bent's death on January 20 and learned that a large force of "rebels" was advancing toward the capital. Price hastily organized his forces, and on the 23rd marched north from Santa Fe with nearly four hundred troops and several pieces of artillery that would prove instrumental in the battles that ensued. Price's force included a company of volunteers under Ceran St. Vrain recruited from among the American merchants, Santa Fe Trail freighters, and others who were at the capital when Price received news of the insurrection.

The following day, January 24, Colonel Price's forces engaged and dispersed a force of approximately 1,500 New Mexicans at Santa Cruz de La Cañada. The official report of the encounter tells us the American troops suffered two men killed and six wounded, while thirty-six "rebels" were killed. In the meantime, the insurgent forces retreated to the strategic gorge of the Rio Grande at Embudo, along the principal route to Taos. On the 27th, Price advanced to Los Luceros and two days later, engaged the New Mexican forces between La Joya (Velarde) and Embudo. When the smoke cleared, the American forces controlled the pass, and the New Mexicans retreated to Taos, where they regrouped and fortified themselves at the Pueblo of San Geronimo de Taos. Casualty reports for the battle at Embudo show that approximately twenty New Mexicans were killed and sixty wounded, while one of the American troops was killed and one severely wounded.

While Colonel Price and his troops were engaging the New Mexican forces at Santa Cruz and Embudo, several Americans were killed on the east side of the Sangre de Cristo Mountains near Mora. A force of American troops stationed at Las Vegas responded to the attacks by assaulting the settlement of Mora on January 24. Their initial assault was repulsed by the New Mexicans, but a week later the United States forces returned to Mora, and on February 1, mounted a devastating artillery barrage that forced the New Mexicans to abandon their positions in the town. The American troops then entered Mora and proceeded to raze the community to the ground. At least twenty-five New Mexicans were reported killed in these actions. The fate of several prisoners whom the Americans took at Mora is unknown.

Figure 28. "The Battle of Mora, N. M., February 1, 1847." Twitchell, *History of the Military Occupation*, 137.

A Ruthless Suppression

The events that are commonly known as the "Revolt of 1847" began on January 19, 1847, with the assassination of Governor Charles Bent at Taos. As we have seen in the previous article, the response of American military commander Colonel Sterling Price was quick and decisive. After the American military routed the insurrectionists at Santa Cruz de la Cañada and Embudo, New Mexican forces retreated and regrouped at San Geronimo de Taos. During this same period, American troops out of Las Vegas had assaulted Mora and razed the village to the ground.

On the west side of the Sangre de Cristo Mountains, Colonel Price and his troops advanced on Taos and on February 3, reached the settlement of Don Fernando and commenced an artillery barrage on the Pueblo of Taos, where the New Mexicans

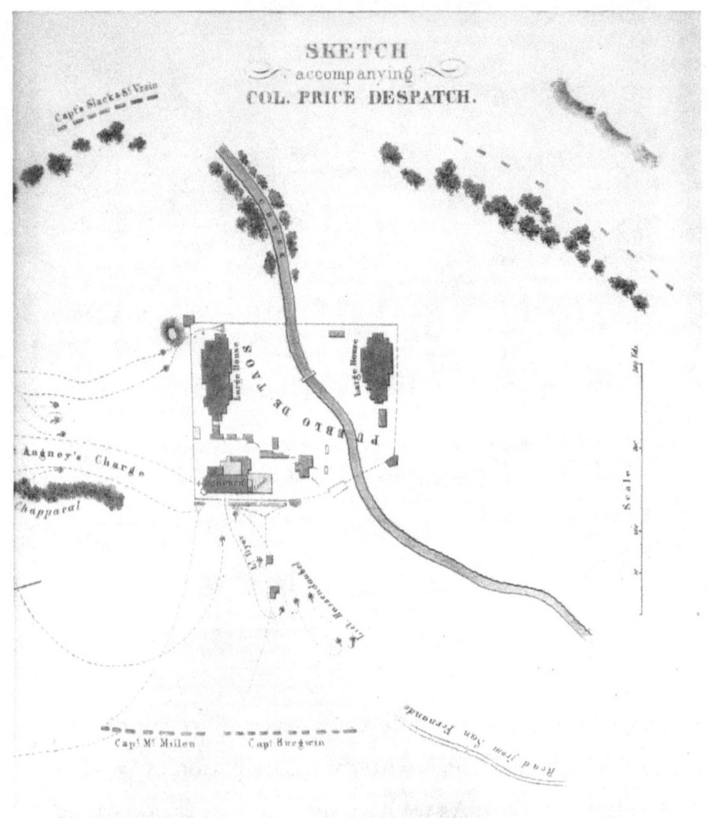

Figure 29. Plan of battle at the Pueblo of Taos. "Insurrection Against the Military Government in New Mexico and California, 1847 and 1848" Senate Document No. 442, 65th Congress, 1st Session. Cited in Michael McNierney. *Taos 1847, The Revolt in Contemporary Accounts* (Johnson Publishing Company, 1980), 72–73.

and their Pueblo Indian allies had fortified themselves. Late the following morning, Price's troops began their assault on the pueblo along two fronts. The Americans managed to fight their way past the outer defenses but were unable to dislodge the New Mexicans from behind the adobe walls of the church of San Geronimo, which provided a large measure of protection from the artillery.

Finally, at three o'clock, the afternoon of February 4, the Americans wheeled the largest gun they had—a six pounder—to within sixty yards of the church and began to batter the wall at a spot where an earlier attempt to chop through with axes had been beaten back. When the wall was breached, the cannon was brought up to point-blank range, and several rounds of grape shot were poured into the hole.

The onslaught was too much for the outgunned defenders to resist, and a general rout ensued as the Americans stormed through the breach. As several hundred Mexicans and Pueblo allies attempted to escape, Ceran St. Vrain's volunteers pursued those who had fled and apparently did so enthusiastically, killing more than fifty "rebels" before they reached the safety of the nearby hills. Various sources estimate that between 150 and 200 defenders died at the pueblo, bringing the total number of New Mexicans who died on the battlefields of northern New Mexico to nearly 300, although the actual number will likely never be known. Pablo Montoya, Tomas Romero, and several dozen survivors were captured. Romero, identified as one of the principal leaders in the insurrection, was killed the following day, shot by a nervous guard while allegedly trying to escape.

We know little of what became of the several hundred individuals killed at Taos or the battles at Santa Cruz and Embudo. Burial records tell us the names of a few who managed to receive an ecclesiastic burial, but dozens were apparently buried anonymously in unknown and unmarked graves. Indications are, several women may have also been killed. The *St. Louis (Mo.) Daily Republican* report of the battle suggests casualties among the women who carried water to the defenders and cared for the wounded. Philip St. George Cooke, a participant in the battle, wrote that "In the heat of the assault, a dragoon was in the act of killing a woman, unrecognized by dress, similar to the man's, and both sexes wearing the hair long; in this extremity she saved her life by an act of the most conclusive personal exposure!"

On February 6, a mere two days following the battle at the Pueblo of Taos, Colonel Price convened a military court to try Pablo Montoya and several unnamed individuals for their part in the revolt. Three separate charges were lodged against Montoya. The first was that on January 19, 1847, Montoya "did . . . excite the Indians and Mexicans to rebellious conduct." Second, that on January 25, 1847, he had issued a proclamation "exciting the people to rebellion," and finally, that he had conspired to "rob United States wagons loaded with public funds." While it is possible to interpret these charges as being synonymous with treason, contrary to many published sources, the word "treason" does not appear in the charges brought against Pablo Montoya.

Justice was dispensed quickly to Pablo Montoya. He was indicted, tried, convicted, and sentenced to hang, all on that first day of court. According to the death warrant issued by Colonel

Price, Montoya was hanged on February 7, 1847, sometime between eleven in the morning and two o'clock that afternoon, "in the centre of the plaza" of Don Fernando. Thus ended the first stage of the ruthless justice imposed on the leaders of that insurrection known as the "Revolt of 1847."

The "Treason Trials" of 1847

Following Pablo Montoya's execution at Taos on February 7, 1847, the scene shifted to Santa Fe, where a grand jury was convened on March 8. This jury returned indictments for "High Treason" against four men believed to be the principal leaders and organizers of what has come to be known as the "Revolt of 1847."

The first indictment in these "Treason Trials" was against Antonio María Trujillo of Los Luceros. The long and elegantly handwritten indictment charges that Trujillo, "withdrawing the allegiance, fidelity & obedience which every true and faithful citizen of the United States should & of right ought to bear towards the [government of the United States] . . . most wickedly & traitorously did levy and make war against the said government."

On March 12, Trujillo was tried, convicted of the charges, and four days later sentenced to hang. Judge Joab Houghton's sentence is the earliest and one of the most famous of the many condemnations, or "death sentences" pronounced by New Mexico's territorial judiciary. One can imagine the hush that descended over the courtroom as Judge Houghton addressed the condemned prisoner who stood before him:

> Your age and grey (sic) hairs have excited the sympathy of both the Court and the jury. . . . Yet have you been found guilty of the crime alleged to your charge. It would appear that old age has not brought you wisdom nor purity or honesty of heart. . . . You have nourished bitterness and hatered (sic) in your soul. You have been found seconding the acts of a band of the most traitorous murderers that ever blackened with the recital of their deeds the annals of history. . . .
>
> For such foul crimes, an enlightened and liberal jury have been compelled from the evidence . . . and by a sense of their stern but unmistakable duty, to find you guilty of treason against the government *under which you are a citizen* [emphasis added]. And there only remains to the court the painful duty of passing upon you the sentence of the law, which is, that you be taken hence to prison, there to remain until Friday the 16th of April next and that at 2 o'clock in the afternoon of that day you be taken thence to the place of execution and there be hanged by the neck till you are dead! dead! dead! And may the Almighty God have mercy on your soul.

In the days following Trujillo's trial and conviction, the three other men indicted by the grand jury for treason, Pantaleón Archuleta of Los Luceros, Trinidad Barcelo of Santa Fe, and Pedro Vigil of Trampas, were also brought to trial. But all three resulted in hung juries, and by the time court adjourned in early May, charges against all three were dropped.

There are several reasons for this turn of events. However, the principal reason is based on the appeal filed on Trujillo's behalf, which questioned the authority of an American court to try a

Mexican citizen for treason against the United States. Within days, many individuals, including the United States district attorney who prosecuted the case and members of the jury who convicted him, joined in support of a petition to the President of the United States requesting a suspension of the sentence and pardon for Trujillo.

However, there is no evidence that Trujillo was directly pardoned by President Polk. Secretary of war, W. L. Marcy, acknowledged that it was probably not "proper use of the legal term" to convict Mexican citizens as traitors to the United States and apparently authorized Colonel Sterling Price, as military governor, to use his own discretion as to whether Trujillo should be pardoned. A diligent search has found no primary evidence of Trujillo's execution or of a burial that would have presumably followed such an execution. There is also no record of any official actions taken by Colonel Price in the matter, and in the absence of evidence of a presidential pardon, all indications are that Price subsequently exercised the pardon informally and ordered Trujillo released.

Several histories of the period support this theory. Thomas Hart Benton, the long-serving senator from Missouri who was in a position to know these things, wrote that a pardon presented a quandary for President Polk because the court that convicted Trujillo clearly had "no jurisdiction for treason." A pardon would have meant the United States government supported "the legality of the condemnation" and if no pardon was issued an execution would "subject [Trujillo] to murder." According to Benton, a compromise was reached by which Trujillo was simply released. Twenty-five others being held prisoner in Santa Fe were also discharged at this time, according to one official, "for want of testimony to indict them for treason."

But New Mexico's introduction to American jurisprudence did not end with Trujillo's release and acquittal of his compatriots. When the court adjourned in Santa Fe, the scene once again shifted to Taos, where the most brutal reprisals against the insurrectionists would take place.

The Trials at Taos

While Antonio María Trujillo and his compatriots were being tried in Santa Fe in March of 1847, more than forty men—possibly the ones captured with Pablo Montoya that past February—were still being held prisoner at Taos. To deal with them, a civil court convened there on April 5. Judge Charles Beaubien, whose son was killed in Taos at the onset of the revolt on January 19, presided. George Bent, brother of the recently assassinated governor, served as foreman of the grand jury. Among the first indictments were Polio Salazar and Francisco "Rovali" [Ulibarri], charged with "high treason" against the United States. On April 7, Beaubien's court convicted Polio Salazar of treason and sentenced him to hang. Francisco Ulibarri, the other person indicted with Salazar for treason, was acquitted of the charge a few days later—possibly by then the court had learned that it had no jurisdiction for treason. With Ulibarri's acquittal and Antonio María Trujillo's earlier release, Polio Salazar gained the dubious distinction of being the only person executed for treason as a result of the events that have become known as the "Treason Trials of 1847."

In an obvious change of tactics, the court singled out and indicted at least sixteen of the prisoners held at Taos for murder (instead of treason) in the killing of Governor Bent and other American officials. Five men—José Manuel García, Pedro Lucero, Juan Ramón Trujillo, Manuel Romero, and Isidro Romero—were convicted of the murder charge and all five were sentenced to hang with Polio Salazar on April 9.

Official records provide no details of the April 9 executions. Catholic Church burial records simply tell us that Padre Antonio José Martínez buried five of the six the same day they were hanged. The individual burial entries note that they each received the last Sacraments of the Church before their judicial sentence was carried out.

The most complete account of the events of that fateful day of April 9, comes from Lewis H. Garrard's book, *Wah-To-Yah and the Taos Trail.* Garrard's eyewitness story describes the men's final walk from the jail to a gallows, where a wagon was driven under a crossbeam that had been fastened to two upright poles. The six condemned men were positioned carefully on a thick plank placed across the rear of the wagon. After the ropes were adjusted around their neck, each was allowed to say a few words to the sparse crowd that had gathered. After the condemned men bade each other farewell, the wagon was driven out from under them. As their bodies swayed back and forth, two of them managed to grasp hands, and for a few moments, held on to each other in a desperate grip, until unconsciousness, and then death, overtook them. It is possible that these two were Manuel Antonio Romero and Isidro Antonio Romero, who may have been cousins, if not brothers.

On April 12, three days after Polio Salazar and his companions were buried, the appalling spectacle of the executions prompted Padre Martínez to send a runner to Santa Fe with two letters. The first was addressed to Manuel Álvarez, a prominent merchant and United States consul at the capital. Padre Martínez informed Álvarez that Charles Beaubien, the presiding judge, seemed intent on killing everyone in Taos. If the executions continued, there would soon be no one left to plant fields at this critical time of the year. Padre Martínez pleaded with Álvarez to accompany the runner when he delivered the other letter to Colonel Sterling Price and do what he could to put a stop to the suffering at Taos.

Padre Martínez's second letter, addressed to Colonel Price, is a poignant appeal for mercy and a condemnation of the proceedings in Taos. Besides the trials being held in English because the prosecuting and defense attorneys did not speak Spanish, Martínez noted that the juries that condemned those being tried, were "a class of ignorant men . . . tainted with passion." The trials and executions at Taos had deteriorated into a "frightful spectacle" that was causing general discontent and resentment. There is no record of Price's response, and the trials and executions at Taos continued.

The extant court records show that there were ten additional convictions for murder before the court adjourned at Taos. All ten received sentences of death by hanging. Nine of this group were sentenced to hang on April 30, and the tenth scheduled for

May 7. We have no official record of these final ten executions, and church burial records for Taos confirm only two burials from this group. However, William B. Drescher, one of the Missouri Volunteers who marched to New Mexico with General Kearny in August 1846, has left us his account of the executions of the nine men sentenced to hang on April 30. As with the earlier executions, the condemned men were placed on wagons that were driven under the gallows. If all ten of these final hangings were carried out as scheduled, they brought the total number of executions from the April 1847 Taos Trials to seventeen.

Tragedy at Los Valles

When the court closed at Taos on April 24, 1847, it appeared that New Mexico's harsh introduction to American jurisprudence had come to an end. But the summer of 1847 brought more tragedy. In early July 1847, the bodies of a Lieutenant Brown and two enlisted men were discovered near Los Valles, about twenty miles south of Las Vegas. Brown and his men had been missing since late June, and suspicion immediately fell upon the residents of this isolated community. Warranted or not, reprisals were quick. On or about July 6, 1847, a detachment of American troops descended on Los Valles and literally erased the community from the face of the earth. Within hours, at least six of Los Valles's residents lay dead, and nearly every building in the village destroyed. At least forty men were taken prisoner and marched to Santa Fe to stand trial for killing Lieutenant Brown and his men.

On July 26 Colonel Sterling Price convened a "drumhead court martial" for seven men singled out for trial. Of this group, Manuel Alvarado was acquitted and presumably released, but the other six were convicted and sentenced to hang. The executions of José Tomás Duran, George Rodríguez, Manual Saens, Pedro Martín, Carpio Martín, and Dionicio Martín were carried out on August 3, 1847. As the men were hanged, an observer noted that all of Santa Fe's church bells tolled, sounding an end to the events we generally associate with the "Revolt" and "Treason Trials" of 1847.

During January and February 1847, three hundred or more New Mexicans were killed in battles with the American invaders. Between February and August, twenty-one men were executed on charges of murder—one for treason, and another on the dubious charge of fomenting "rebellious conduct." The death of so many in so short a time undoubtedly carried serious consequences. The old San Geronimo church was in ruins, and no doubt the Pueblo of Taos had incurred severe damage. The communities of Mora and Los Valles were also in ruins and the villages around Santa Cruz and along the valley of Embudo may have been deserted. Hundreds of men were dead and scores were undoubtedly seriously impaired by wounds. Dozens of widows and possibly hundreds of orphans were left without proper care and support. Will we ever know how this great loss of men as spring approached impacted the ability of these communities to plant the crops needed for their subsistence?

We know almost nothing about the motives of the men who decided to take up arms and died in this insurrection against the Americans in 1847. Were their actions motivated

Figure 30. Ruins of the San Geronimo church, Pueblo of Taos, no date. Johnson's Studio, Dawson, New Mexico, postcard. Robert J. Tórrez Collection.

by patriotism, hate, fear, or some other reason? How about the motives of those who supported the new American government? Men of influence who wrote of these events soon after they had occurred used derogatory terms to describe those who had taken up arms against the United States in January 1847. A newspaper report of a dance given by Colonel Sterling Price at the Palace of the Governors on the first anniversary of the battle at Taos, described the occasion as a celebration of the "complete extinction of the band of murderers who under the pretense of patriotism killed and robbed so many defenseless innocents." Others have alluded to these men, and New Mexicans in general, as "miserable, ignorant, deluded wretches . . . so degraded . . .

that they are wholly unfit to be citizens of a free government." Territorial Secretary William G. Ritch, in his eloquent eulogy of Donaciano Vigil, attributed the events of 1847 to the "discontent and dissentions among the Pueblos and the more ignorant and vicious classes in remote districts." More recently, prominent and respected authors dismissed these New Mexicans as little more than "young hot-headed *caballeros* who had declined to swear allegiance to the new country."

There are many more such characterizations of New Mexicans through the late nineteenth and early twentieth centuries. History has, and regrettably continues, to label those who participated in these tragic events of 1847 as rebels and traitors despite the officially acknowledged fact that the courts convened in Taos and Santa Fe had no authority to condemn Mexican citizens for treason against the United States. When labeled with such vicious descriptions, no wonder these men have been considered undeserving of any recognition or honor. It may finally be time to suggest that instead of the disgraceful anonymity in which these events have been held by history, we now dare to consider whether the events of those dark days of late December 1846, through August 1847, should even be called a "revolt." Would "insurrection" or "resistance" be more appropriate? It may be time to face the challenge of considering that the men and women who died resisting the American invasion during those fateful days in 1847 should be worthy of being remembered and honored, not as rebels and traitors, but as Mexican patriots who died defending their country.

Author's note

Details of the US occupation and response to the 1847 insurrection are taken principally from the following sources: "Occupation of Mexican Territory, Message from the President of the United States, December 22, 1846," House of Representatives Executive Document No. 19, 29th Congress, 2nd Session, 1846–1847 (Serial No. 499); "Insurrection Against the Military Government in New Mexico and California in 1847 and 1848," Senate Document 442, 56th Congress, 1st Session (Serial No. 3878); US District Court Records, Federal Records Center, Denver, Colorado; 1st. Judicial District, New Mexico, Criminal Case Files, 1847–1865; *Microfilm Edition of the Land Records of New Mexico: Spanish Archives of New Mexico, Series I* (New Mexico State Records Center and Archives, 1987); and Records of the Adjutant General's Office (RG94), Orders and Special Orders, Vol. 43 1/2, Army of New Mexico, 1847, 9th Military Department. National Archives Microfilm.

Glossary

This glossary consists of selected Spanish words or terms utilized in the texts of these pages. While most of the Spanish words or terms used herein have provided a short definition or meaning in parenthesis when they appear in the texts, the following are Spanish words and terms that may require a fuller definition or explanation.

alcalde: Generally defined, it refers to a civil official serving at the local level with judicial, executive, and often military authority in the militia under the additional title of capitán de guerra. The alcalde mayor is the superior official in charge of a district often referred to as an alcaldía, a geographical region that extended beyond a municipality to include surrounding communities that can be compared to a contemporary county. The alcalde mayor was assisted in his duties by officers referred to by various terms, such as *alcalde ordinario*, who served at the municipal level or alcalde de barrio, who served within a district or precinct in the municipality.

alférez: A military rank typically defined as a standard or flag bearer, a rank below that of capitán (captain) and teniente (lieutenant). Presidio musters often list more than one alférez, a *primero* (first) and segundo (second), probably based on seniority. These are followed in rank by what we might consider the non-commissioned officers of *sergento* (sergeant) and cabo (corporal), followed by carabinero (carabineer), *armero* (armorer or gunsmith), and *soldado* (soldier). A number of documents apply the term capitán or capitancillo to individuals we would consider chiefs or leaders of the various frontier tribes.

casas reales: The term typically applied to the complex or grouping of official government buildings that included the governor's house, commonly referred to as the Palace of the Governors, and adjacent buildings or rooms associated with judicial or administrative officers and the military.

cepo (also *sepo* or *zepo*): Stocks used for punishment. No descriptions of these devices have been located in the archives, but they were probably similar to the wooden stocks that often illustrate the punishment devices utilized by the Puritan forefathers. In New Mexico the use of stocks may have been more for preventing escape from confinement than for punishment. It is also not certain they were attached to a vertical pole. This type of device seems to have been more often used for the legs than for the arms and head, although on several occasions, sentences specified that prisoners were to be placed *de cabeza en el sepo*. An 1828 inventory lists twelve sets of grillos and two pairs of *grilletes* at the *sala de armas* (armory). Another type of confinement was the *corma*, where the person's feet were bound to a beam or board with rope or rawhide because grillos were not available. The term *bien cormado* is sometimes found in documents when officials are advised that a prisoner needed to be well secured, especially while he was being transported.

estranjero: Technically a stranger, but more typically refers to a foreigner. It is commonly used to refer to Americans, Frenchmen, and people of other nationalities who entered New Mexico.

fanega: A unit of dry volume used to measure crops, such as wheat or corn. As with the vara, the official volume of a fanega was undefined during the Spanish era but was based on examples or dimensions provided to local authorities by Spanish officials. In 1852 the New Mexico territorial legislature officially defined the *media fanega* (one-half fanega) as 2,476 1/4 cubic inches, making the full fanega the approximate volume of 2.303 bushels. Twelve almudes constituted a full fanega.

gefe politico: The official title for the individual commonly referred to as governor. This title applies to the individual in charge of the civil government to differentiate it from the office of comandante general or comandante principal, a position held by the commanding officer of the Santa Fe presidio military garrison. Some governors, such as Manuel Armijo, held both offices, giving them civil and military authority. It should be noted that whomever held the civil and/or military office in New Mexico was subordinate to the comandante general in Chihuahua.

grillos: Shackles or irons, as in *un par de grillos* (a pair of shackles). The hardware consisted of two shackles attached by a short chain. They seem to have been normally used for the ankles, but occasionally, documents specify that especially combative prisoners or those prone to escape were to be confined with two pairs, implying that they were to be used to bind the arms and legs. A smaller version, probably used only for the wrists, are sometimes referred to as grilletes. An 1805 inventory of the property found in the Santa Fe presidio shows that they had four pairs of grillos and one grillete.

guia: A passport issued to American and Mexican traders transporting goods between New Mexico and other Mexican provinces. These typically listed an inventory of the items being shipped, their valuation, and the fees, or tariffs, paid.

invalido: A retired soldier often listed on presidio musters as part of the garrison with a pension. Soldiers earned this status due to a physical infirmity or service-connected injury that limited their ability to serve effectively in the military.

jusgado (also juzgado): The courtroom or place where judicial proceedings took place. The term is not used to indicate a jail, although the anglicized term "hoosegow" usually implies a jail. A typical context in which judicial officials used the term was when an alcalde summoned someone to appear before them, such as *lo hice comparecer en este mi jusgado* (I ordered [them] to appear in this my court). The term also appears as a verb, indicating that an individual was judged.

matachines: The term describes traditional dancing troupes such as those featured in the 1822 Iturbide celebration. These dances were performed by adult men and children, dramatizing encounters between the Spanish, Aztecs, Moors, and in some contemporary New Mexico settlements and pueblos, the Comanches.

moso: A servant or employee. Mosos are often referred to in the context of a resident servant who lives in the household or otherwise serving the amo, or master of a household. Individuals typically identify themselves or are described as "moso de" such and such a person or family for whom they work. Many references to mosos relate to debts owed by the moso to his or her amo, suggesting that these individuals were in situations of debt servitude.

peón: A laborer. The term is typically used to describe a worker who is not a skilled tradesman. Tradesmen are often identified as a maestro (master) of a particular trade or simply by their specific trade such as an *adobero* (maker of adobes), *albanil* (mason), *carpintero* (carpenter) or other term specific to his trade. Documents typically show that peones were paid a daily wage that was less than those of a tradesman.

peso: The silver Spanish and Mexican coin with a value of *ocho* (eight) reales. These coins were not stamped with "un peso" value but as "8 reales." The Mexican government issued coins with eight, four, one, one-half, and even one-fourth real denominations.

presidio: Technically presidios were garrisoned fortifications established along hostile frontiers of New Spain, but the term is generally applied to the site where a paid garrison of soldiers was stationed. There were two presidios in Spanish-era New Mexico, the original in Paso del Norte, established during the decades-long absence of the Spanish from New Mexico following the Pueblo Revolt of 1680, and the one established in the villa of Santa Fe following the reconquista of 1692 and that functioned, often in a limited capacity, until 1846.

ranchería: A collection of huts or temporary buildings. The term was typically applied to a site where the Navajos or other tribal group had a small, possibly temporary settlement or encampment consisting of *hoganes*, tepees, or other shelters.

regidor: A serving member of the ayuntamientos, the municipal councils that are mentioned many times within these pages. These served under the alcalde mayor and took turns performing certain functions as regidores de cano, a sort of councilman of the day.

rescate: A form of the Spanish word for rescue or ransom by purchase or exchange. Rescates were official regulated opportunities (commonly called "trade fairs") to trade with the various frontier tribes.

tonterías: Foolishness, as used in the diary of a conference held by Governor José Antonio Chaves with Comanche leaders at Bosque Redondo in 1829. The Comanche leaders agreed to do their best to keep their young men from committing tonterías, likely referring to thefts of livestock or raids on communities. Readers may recall the term last used when their parents cautioned them about indulging in certain foolishness at Saturday night dances.

vara: A staff or rod issued to alcaldes as a symbol of their authority. It also served as the ubiquitous unit of measure whose official length was undefined during the Spanish era but established by examples issued by Spanish authorities to local governments. The Mexican government established the official length of the *vara Mexicana* (Mexican vara) at 838 mm in 1846, which is generally considered to be the equivalent of thirty-three inches. The vara Mexicana was slightly shorter than the Spanish-era *vara castellana* or *vara de Burgos*.

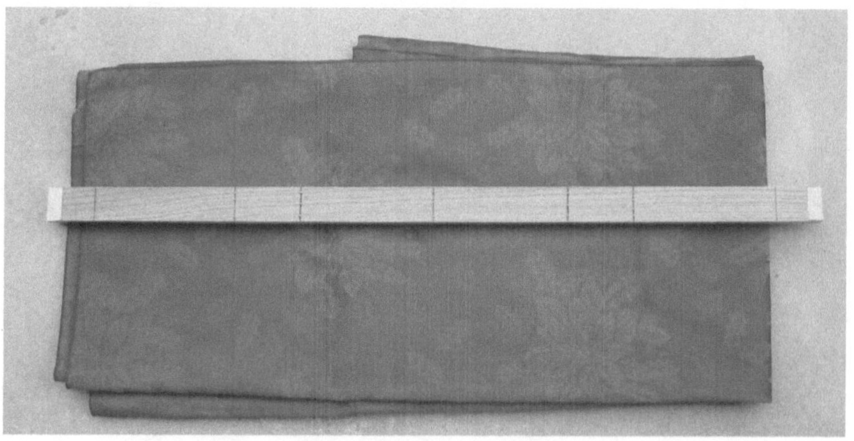

Figure 31. The author's personal vara constructed to the 1846 Mexican standard 838 mm. The markings designate the one half, one third, one fourth, and one sixteenth portions of the standard vara.

villa: A term that identifies a community with elevated status, such as a seat of government. New Mexico had three communities that were given this important status—the villa of Santa Fe, which retained that status from its founding in 1610; Santa Cruz de la Cañada, the first settlement established following the reconquista of 1692–1693; and Albuquerque in 1706.

vocal: A serving member of the governing council or provincial (as in the entire province of New Mexico) legislature designated originally in 1822 as the *Diputación Provincial,* or simply diputación. The terminology changed as new Mexican constitutions were implemented. The diputación became the Junta Departamental in 1835, and finally, the Asamblea Departamental in 1842. The primer vocal assumed the functions of the gefe politico (governor) in his absence.

www.ingramcontent.com/pod-product-compliance
Lightning Source LLC
LaVergne TN
LVHW091123080826
845145LV00008B/2025